THE Small Business Savings Plan

101 Tactics for Controlling Costs and Boosting the Bottom Line

TIMOTHY R. GASE

KAPLAN

PUBLISHING

New York

This publication is designed to provide accurate and authoritative information in regard to the subject matter covered. It is sold with the understanding that the publisher is not engaged in rendering legal, accounting, or other professional service. If legal advice or other expert assistance is required, the services of a competent professional should be sought.

Editorial Director: Jennifer Farthing
Acquisitions Editor: Shannon Berning
Development Editor: Joshua Martino
Production Editor: Julio Espin
Production Artist: Todd Bowman
Cover Designer: Kathleen Lynch, Rod Hernandez

Published by Kaplan Publishing,
a division of Kaplan, Inc.

Printed in the United States of America

May 2007
07 08 09 10 9 8 7 6 5 4 3 2 1

ISBN-13: 978-1-4195-9391-8
ISBN-10: 1-4195-9391-9

For information about ordering Kaplan Publishing books at special quantity discounts, please call 1-800-KAP-ITEM or write to Kaplan Publishing, 888 Seventh Ave., 22nd floor, New York, NY 10106.

Contents

There are so many people I would like to thank for their help in giving me the inspiration to put this book together . . . and for the ideas themselves. It starts with my parents, who taught me that hard work and good morals would take me a long way in life.

There isn't a car dealer or appliance salesperson I've met whom my mother couldn't out-haggle for a great deal. She's always been there for support, whether it was consoling me after a tough loss playing baseball as a kid or dealing with a tough personnel issue today.

My father was a finish carpenter who always worked hard and expected the same from those around him. As you can imagine, he expected things to be done in an efficient, yet very professional, manner. He had a saying posted on the wall of his shop, "No job is complete until you clean up your mess." He saved everything that was left over from his remodeling jobs, thinking he would have some opportunity to cut costs using these things on some future job.

He built a home shortly before he passed away and did all the work himself, from running the wire to making his own kitchen cabinets. I stopped by a number of times while he was building the house; he would take me through each room and brag about how much he had saved on some special buy he'd discovered for the lights, the wire, the bathtub, the carpeting, or the shingles on the roof. He truly enjoyed trying to find ways to save a buck and do things more efficiently. So it's obvious where I get my drive.

Thanks to my wife, Jan, for being the catalyst that holds our family together, from making sure our finances are in order to seeing that the kids have done their homework. Without her, I would be lost. She is always encouraging and supportive in whatever I do. Having your wife as your best friend makes life so much simpler when you're looking for a second opinion. As you'll see, she's also cut from the same mold as I am, in that her parents were very frugal while she was growing up.

I have two wonderful children, Michael and Stephanie, whom I look forward to seeing every evening when I return from work. I love hearing about each new adventure that takes place at school each day. They are just awesome kids; you make your dad proud.

I need to thank my business partner, Ken, for being there for support when we had the opportunity to buy the company. It's been a good partnership. We've had our bumps in the road, but we are a good team. I tend to be the risk taker, and he's a bit more conservative, bringing me back to reality to think things through.

Thanks to all my Chief Executive Board International (CEBI) buddies. You guys are awesome. I've known some of these small business owners for nearly eight years. They have been a great support team and a source for many of the ideas in this book.

I want to thank my Scotch Club buddies for their support, especially Dan, who helped me through my first edit. I owe you a bottle of 18-year-old Glenlivet for that one.

To my editor, Bruce, thanks for making the process of writing this book relatively painless and for making my simple words sound so much better.

And finally, Kaplan Publishing, thanks for believing in my idea for this book and giving me the means to share my ideas with other businesses in the hope I can help them survive to fight another day.

This book is the accumulation of nearly 20 years of cost-saving ideas that I have either applied in my own business or learned about from other small business owners and executives. Don't expect to find fancy pricing strategies or complex formulas for reducing shrinkage. Economics and business professors have plenty to offer in those areas. What I will offer isn't rocket science. Instead, it's common sense combined with one part savvy and one part ingenuity. I suspect that you may have already put at least a few of these ideas into practice in your business. What this book does, though, is share the great ideas that other business owners have come up with. To my knowledge, no one has ever collected all these cost-saving tips and techniques and presented them in one place.

Many resources explain ways to improve business profitability using sophisticated costing systems. As effective as these systems may be, they usually are more appropriate for big corporations than for small companies. Within these pages, you're not going to find any scientific formulas. Instead, you'll find "tricks of the trade." Most business owners I know, including some of those who contributed ideas to this book, possess a few cost-cutting tricks they've learned over the years that have helped them excel in business or at least remain competitive. These tricks vary from cutting insurance costs to decreasing your annual postage bill, from capitalizing on employee benefits savings to doing all sorts of things to retain employees who both make and save the company money.

NECESSITY IS THE MOTHER OF INVENTION

I have no doubt that if I had not created and used some of the ideas you'll find in these pages, my business would have gone under. I was driven to find ways to reduce expenses because my business demanded it. As I implemented some new practices to cut costs, I was astonished at how well these ideas worked. It struck me that if I could do it, anyone could, and that if I had a few great ways to reduce costs and save dollars, other small company executives would probably also have some terrific concepts that they had put into practice. As a small business owner myself, I know the unique challenges of running your own business, and I felt compelled to share this knowledge. That's the short version of why I wrote this book.

I've worked in manufacturing for the past 20 years. I received my undergraduate degree in business at Ohio University. I went back eight years later and received an EMBA in 1992, a two-year program that was directed at students with seven or more years of professional experience. I learned as much from the other students as I did from the professors. Those were two tough years of all-day Saturday classes, especially while I was working full-time, but it was a great program that taught the importance of learning from my peers.

After graduating from college, I worked for Cooper Industries, the Apex Division of Cooper Power Tools, located in Dayton, Ohio. We manufactured industrial screwdriver bits and sockets used on automotive and heavy equipment assembly lines. We also produced universal joints for industrial and many military applications. In my 12 years there, I held eight different job titles, all at the same plant. I started out as a management trainee working in the industrial engineering office, then became a foreperson in a department of 30 UAW employees, 20 of whom were women. I also spent some time in sales as a product line manager and sales rep contact for all sales west of the Mississippi River. Prior to leaving

Cooper, I had direct profit and loss responsibility for the universal joint product line, which proved to be a great experience.

In 1995, I left Cooper to take a job as president of a Columbus, Ohio-based manufacturing business, Peerless Saw Company, which was owned by a Finnish company. In my fifth year with the company, the CEO called and said that we were going to be sold to another company in our industry. I realized that I might not have a job if the deal went through. It occurred to me that I might be able to put together a management buyout, and when I asked him if he would consider such a buyout, he told me that he would.

I bought the company with a partner in September of 1999, and we have done well. Initially, however, we faced a challenging situation. We had bought the company when the economy was at an all-time high and then had to struggle through a serious economic downturn for the next three years. Had we not been meticulous about saving and spending money, it's debatable whether we would have made it.

As you may know, U.S. manufacturers are a dying breed. An economist recently suggested that only 5 percent of the goods used in the United States are actually manufactured here. Today our company is competing against companies in other countries that have all types of competitive advantages, including a cheap labor workforce, lower fringe benefit structures, fewer government restrictions, and fewer legal concerns. We are also competing against huge manufacturers who have economy of scale advantages. It became clear to me early on that if we were going to do well, we needed to manufacture our own advantage.

From the very beginning of our ownership, Peerless was in a very mature market: custom-fabricated industrial saw blades. The technology we use hasn't changed significantly for a number of years, and we don't anticipate any major changes in the near future. We face low prices and a shrinking market. Fortunately, customers like to have a choice, so approximately 90 percent of the products we make are custom-designed to our customers' specifications.

We have 50 employees; 15 are salaried and 35 are hourly. Our wages are average for the area, and our benefit package is a bit above average. Our products are made from imported steel because none of the steel companies in the United States makes the material we use. The company has been in business for over 75 years, and we are only the fourth owners. Our newest employee has worked for us less than a year, but one employee has been with the company for 50 years—and I don't see this individual retiring any time soon.

I have given you a fairly detailed picture of our business to help you understand that we, like most small businesses, face our own set of problems, challenges, and limitations. I have no doubt that there are better businesses to be in—industries with higher margins, more opportunities for expansion, or fewer competitors.

Nonetheless, we have done well. While I don't discount factors such as hard work, highly productive employees, good strategy, and sound management, I know that none of those factors would have mattered if we weren't extraordinarily smart about controlling our costs. At some point, I sat back and realized that we had managed to weather the toughest of times while other companies in the field had not, primarily because of our savvy money-saving approach. I also suspected that we were not alone. How many other small companies had formulated their own cost-saving ideas and managed to come out on top?

I decided to investigate, and the more small business owners I talked to, the more I realized that we all were cost conscious in different ways and that we had helped our companies save money in just about every organizational area.

However, I also was aware that many small business owners fail to save and spend wisely. In a recent trade publication, I read that approximately 80 percent of all start-up businesses fail within three years. I also came across an even scarier statistic: 95 percent of start-up companies fail within their first five years of operation. And in the past two years, more companies have faced bankruptcy than ever before. Most of these businesses generally fail for one of two reasons: they lack financial backing to support them through start-up and early growth periods, or they lack good management. With the information in this book, I hope to help owners and managers reduce the costs of operating a business so that they and their companies don't face such a financial burden.

BOTTOM LINE BENEFITS: NEWS YOU CAN USE

As you'll discover, every chapter contains scores of ideas you can apply to your business. Some may save you thousands of dollars annually, while others may help you save $10 here and $20 there. Some may provide you with real dollars that go directly to your bottom line, while other tactics and techniques result in less tangible, though no less significant, financial gains. The chapters are grouped by topic—accounting, utilities, sales and marketing, and so on. This will help you find specific information related to your particular areas of concern. I'll also provide you with as many tools as I can—checklists, questions, red flags—that should make applying these ideas easier. Throughout the book, you'll also find stories illustrating particular points. Some of the stories are from my own experiences, while others have been told to me by other company owners and executives.

Ultimately, all of this will benefit you and your company in a number of ways.

First, it will provide you with numerous options for reducing costs. I'm not claiming every idea in these pages is applicable to your business. You may already be doing some of the things I suggest, or business circumstances may make it impossible for you to implement them. I've found, however, that small business owners often fail to control their costs because they simply aren't aware of the hundreds of possible ways, big and small, in which they could do so. You're going to find a wealth of ideas (pardon the pun) about everything from making salespeople more profitable to making smart purchasing decisions. I've found that the more options small business owners have in this area, the more likely they are to take advantage of them.

Second, this book will motivate you to save money. It's difficult to implement cost-saving concepts if you're not fully convinced that they will have a significant impact on your business. In fact, small business executives are often initially skeptical when I present these ideas, insisting that they're doing everything possible to keep costs down and that anything else they might do would only have token effects. Throughout the book, charts, statistics, and firsthand accounts by small business owners like you will convince you that implementing a frugal advantage strategy is worth it.

For instance, Table 1 shows the bottom line results from reducing costs by a dollar versus obtaining the same bottom-line results due to an increase in sales. If a business is operating at a gross margin of 30 percent and reduces its operating expenses by $1,000, it would have to increase its sales volume by $7,000 to have the same bottom line.

If this chart isn't motivation enough, consider this story. We decided a few years ago to let go an outside salesperson we had in a new territory; he just wasn't performing up to expectations. When we took everything into consideration—wages, car expenses, hotels, meals, it cost us about $100,000 a year to keep this salesperson in place. If he were doing an average or above average job, it certainly would have made sense to keep him. But we had given him plenty of time to deliver decent results, and he was unable to do so. Many small companies are especially leery of dropping salespeople from their staff, since they hope against hope that at any moment, the salesperson will break through and deliver a big account. They rationalize waiting, telling themselves that the salesperson isn't costing them that much and the investment is worth the potential reward. We chose to look at the issue through the motivating lens of the operating costs chart. This meant that unless our sales level were to drop by $700,000 a year,

TABLE I *Adding $1 to the Bottom Line by Cost Reduction versus Increasing Sales Dollars*

GM	$1.00	$1,000	$10,000	$20,000	$35,000	$70,000	$105,000
75%	$1.33	$1,333	$13,333	$26,667	$46,667	$93,333	$140,000
70%	$1.43	$1,429	$14,286	$28,571	$50,000	$100,000	$150,000
65%	$1.54	$1,538	$15,385	$30,769	$53,846	$107,692	$161,538
60%	$1.67	$1,667	$16,667	$33,333	$58,333	$116,667	$175,000
55%	$1.82	$1,818	$18,182	$36,364	$63,636	$127,273	$190,909
50%	$2.00	$2,000	$20,000	$40,000	$70,000	$140,000	$210,000
45%	$2.22	$2,222	$22,222	$44,444	$77,778	$155,556	$233,333
40%	$2.50	$2,500	$25,000	$50,000	$87,500	$175,000	$262,500
35%	$2.86	$2,857	$28,571	$57,143	$100,000	$200,000	$300,000
30%	$3.33	$3,333	$33,333	$66,667	$116,667	$233,333	$350,000
25%	$4.00	$4,000	$40,000	$80,000	$140,000	$280,000	$420,000
20%	$5.00	$5,000	$50,000	$100,000	$175,000	$350,000	$525,000
15%	$6.67	$6,667	$66,667	$133,333	$233,333	$466,667	$700,000
10%	$10.00	$10,000	$100,000	$200,000	$350,000	$700,000	$1,050,000
8%	$12.50	$12,500	$125,000	$250,000	$437,500	$875,000	$1,312,500
6%	$16.67	$16,667	$166,667	$333,333	$583,333	$1,166,667	$1,750,000
4%	$25.00	$25,000	$250,000	$500,000	$875,000	$1,750,000	$2,625,000
2%	$50.00	$50,000	$500,000	$1,000,000	$1,750,000	$3,500,000	$5,250,000

The table above indicates the amount you would have to increase your gross sales to equal certain reductions in your expenses relative to your gross margin (GM).

Example: If your GM is 20% and you were able to reduce your expenses by $1,000, you would need to increase your revenues by $5,000 to have the same impact to your bottom line.

we'd see a significant improvement to our bottom line by letting the employee go. It proved to be the right thing to do.

Third, the book will facilitate implementing cost-saving concepts. I'm not just going to give you a list of all the things you can do to save money in your business; I'm going to make it as easy as possible to put them into practice. I will share stories of how small companies reduced their sales staff without hurting morale or sales; I'll explain how to set up a simple system for cutting your utility costs, from turning out lights to running equipment at the least costly time of day. Many small companies hesitate to reduce expenses because they fear the potential negative impact—angry employees protesting the reductions, a corresponding reduction in quality or service, or a reputation for being cheap. I'll suggest how to deal effectively with these issues as you reduce costs.

Fourth, it will increase your business's profitability. This may seem like an unlikely benefit if you believe in the adage, "You've got to spend money to make money." While it's true that slashing costs randomly and ruthlessly probably won't increase profits, I'm suggesting a more strategic and humanistic approach to cost cutting. If you are frugal in the best sense of the word, you will have more cash either to continue improving your business or invest outside of your business. By implementing this strategy, you lower the break-even point of the business and make it more stable when times are rough, such as during a recession. This mind-set will filter down to the rest of your staff, and as more of your managers practice being savings-conscious, they will implement tactics on their own that eventually contribute to your business's profitability.

Frugality is addictive. When companies develop a savings mentality, employees compete to see who can come up with the next great money-saving idea. A friend of mine, Wayne Brumfield, established a pervasive money-saving mentality at his company, the Muncy Corporation. Because of this mentality, one of his purchasing managers came up with a negotiating strategy with suppliers, amending all contracts to charge freight costs to suppliers. While a few suppliers have asked about the change, others have agreed without protest.

Finally, let me translate these benefits into personal terms. If it takes you eight hours to read this book and you value your time at $300 per hour, then I need to show you at least a $2,400 savings in order to justify your time. I'll be disappointed if you don't realize savings of at least five to ten times that! Obviously, I can't guarantee you anything. But I can share with you the experiences of other small business owners in all types of industries who saved considerable amounts of money by implementing these concepts. As I think you'll find, their stories demonstrate what can be done when you make a commitment to being a cost-conscious businessperson.

FRUGAL VERSUS CHEAP: KEEP THE DIFFERENCE IN MIND

This is a critical distinction: I cannot overemphasize that cheap small business owners end up with cheap companies. Organizations that use shoddy materials to save a few bucks, that reduce staff to the point that their remaining employees are overworked, that pay their employees poorly, that develop a reputation for being skinflints and caring only about cost—these companies are likely doomed.

Being frugal is something else entirely. Perhaps I can best describe it by telling you about my parents-in-law. They were able to raise six kids, send them to college, go on family vacations every year, and retire as millionaires. As a schoolteacher and a family farmer, those are significant accomplishments. They achieved these goals by being frugal. They clipped coupons out of the Sunday paper every week, picked up the aluminum cans along their property and turned them in for cash, and took family vacations traveling the country in a station wagon, towing a pop-up camper. They didn't go out and buy a new car every other year; they took care of their possessions and most of them lasted longer than usual. Today they travel all over the world, but they still are frugal, waiting until travel agents tell them the prices are most reasonable.

In other words, they both spend and save wisely. Consider the difference between a cheap and a frugal small business owner. Let's say the cheap owner sees that the blacktop covering her parking lot is cracking. Though it's unsightly and may eventually make it impossible to park there if the crack widens, she figures the company can live with it for at least a few more years, so she does nothing. She doesn't consider the image this parking lot projects when customers visit or how its shoddy appearance impacts employees. The frugal small business owner, on the other hand, obtains several quotes before repairing the blacktop. One of the suppliers he contacts suggests the cost-saving alternative of resealing the lot now and reblacking it in about five years.

Consider another example. The cheap company executive might buy the least expensive raw material regardless of the quality, where a frugal business owner might bargain for the best price and then negotiate a 2 percent discount for paying invoices within ten days. So now her cost might be the same as the business owner who bought the cheapest material, but she has the better quality material.

In a third example, a penurious company president may reprimand his employees for making personal phone calls, threatening to terminate anyone who is caught talking to friends or family during business hours. He doesn't care that his approach demoralizes his people and makes them less motivated to work hard and remain committed. All he cares about is that he has reduced the phone bill by 10 percent over the previous year.

Our company has also been concerned about rising phone bills. Our frugal approach, however, was to talk to two different providers who told us they could reduce our monthly phone bill from $1,900 month to $1,200 per month. Aside from the cost, though, we were happy with our current phone provider, so our controller talked to them about what the other providers had promised. Our provider came up with an alternative plan for us, we put it into action, and we ended up saving $8,400 annually.

Therefore, when you consider implementing any of the ideas contained in this book, you need to ask yourself the following question:

> *Will this action make me look like Scrooge, or will it help me develop a reputation as a savvy business owner who doesn't waste money?*

When we meet annually with our insurance broker and I talk with him about the benefits we offer our employees, he is flabbergasted. Though he is aware of our savings-oriented philosophy, he recognizes that we are extremely generous in terms of employee benefits. At the same time, we're not generous to a fault. To gain a frugal advantage, you must also take the time and make the effort to be what I term an "informed spender."

Recently, I had a meeting with my banker where we discussed the Check 21 change in the banking industry. This change allows banks to clear checks much more quickly than in the past, diminishing the chance of fraud. I told my banker that I had seen very little change in the time that it took for funds to clear into our account since this new paradigm was put into place. It was still taking three days or longer for deposited funds to show up in our account. Our banker was surprised that I was aware of this information; he told me that he had corporate customers ten times our size who had no idea how long it took their money to clear.

These two examples—our generosity and our financial vigilance—define the type of frugality I'm advocating in these pages.

A DEFENSE AGAINST SUDDEN DOWNTURNS AND CRISES

Even if you're skeptical about this book's ability to help your company increase its profitability, focus on how its lessons can provide you with a cushion when you face tough times. In today's unpredictable business world, a competitor or new technology can emerge virtually overnight and throw us for a loop. Temporarily, at least, our business will suffer. Ideally, our cost consciousness will allow us to weather this storm. When we're reducing and controlling our costs routinely, we are in a much better position to survive setbacks than if we are saving erratically or not at all.

A fabrication company in the Midwest was growing rapidly in 2000, and the CEO decided to invest in a new laser and powder-coating system, spending over $1,500,000 on the equipment.

Within a year after 9/11, he was bankrupt, and the equipment was available at an auction for pennies on the dollar. I know this is true because I was contacted about buying the laser that came out of this facility. Had this CEO taken a more conservative fiscal approach, he might still be in business today. He could have challenged his people to find a way to increase their capacity through productivity improvements, subcontracted some work until they were certain their new business was going to be there in the long haul, added employees and gone to three shifts per day, or bought used equipment for half of what they spent on new machines. In short, they could have given themselves sufficient financial cushion to survive the economic downturn in the wake of 9/11—an economic downturn that companies with a savings plan did survive.

Over the years, I've seen more than one small business owner flush with success begin spending as if this success would continue at the same level forever. Perhaps it's a natural human impulse, but when things are going well for a sustained period of time, it's difficult to plan for a period in which this will not be the case. As a result, these business owners spend appropriately for a company that is never going to experience a downturn. If they kept recording solid years one after the other, their spending patterns would never hurt them. Unfortunately, few companies—especially small ones—can count on this pattern of steady success. As a result, they spend frivolously rather than prudently. They don't take advantage of cost-cutting opportunities, and they don't regularly review their expenditures and think holistically and creatively about how they might reduce expenses without diminishing quality, service, or any other aspect of their business.

At the very least, this book will help you develop this holistic and creative mind-set about how your business spends its money, and if and when the day comes when you lose a key account or suffer some other major setback, you'll be in a great position to survive now and thrive later.

1

THERE'S NO TIME
TO SAVE MONEY LIKE
THE PRESENT

Your business may be having a great year, and the idea of saving money is the furthest thing from your mind. Or maybe in the past you have never been overly concerned with costs, convinced that your business doesn't require that you "pinch pennies" to make a good profit. Whatever the reason, you may still be skeptical about the need to develop a small business savings plan.

If so, I'd like to make the argument for why now is the time to make this a goal. It is more difficult than ever before for small companies to remain profitable. If you were able to get away without a savings plan in the past, it's less likely that you'll be able to get away with it now and in the future. Just as significantly, opportunities that never existed before are arising for small companies with frugal strategies; you should be frugal not just to ensure your business's survival in the event of an economic downturn but because you have more chances to save a lot of money than ever.

I'll examine both the positive and the negative developments that make cost savings essential, but let's start with some relatively recent trends that should throw the fear of not saving money into every small business owner.

A LIST OF REASONS TO START SPENDING LESS AND SAVING MORE

In the Introduction, I noted the Small Business Administration statistic that 95 percent of small businesses fail within the first five years. While it is more difficult to ascertain the failure rate of small companies that have been in existence for many years, every other veteran small business owner knows that it's tougher to do well now than it has ever been. We know this because of the events and trends that have placed increasing financial pressure on all of us.

1. **Foreign competition employing cheap labor.** Today we must compete with companies in China with an average labor rate of $2 per day. Additionally, the Chinese government has been known to help businesspeople launch their operations and then forgive the loans that funded the launch. A business owner I know was buying a product from China by the container and reselling it in the United States. When he visited his Chinese supplier for the first time in six months, he discovered a new plant across the street making the same product. The owner of the new plant was an engineer who had previously worked for the supplier. The engineer explained that the Chinese government had just built the brand-new facility with state-of-the-art equipment and that he had no obligation to repay the government for building the plant. Clearly, some Chinese companies as well as other foreign operations possess a competitive advantage that American companies lack.

2. Rising health care costs. The costs of health care have increased an average of 15 percent or more each year since 2002, with no end in sight. As the demographics of businesses change, the increases can become even steeper. If you are like most employers, you are trying to retain highly skilled employees and eliminate turnover. As the workforce ages, however, the risk to insure them becomes greater, and in turn, health care rates skyrocket.

3. OSHA and other safety regulations. The cost of compliance can tax even the healthiest of businesses. OSHA has helped created safe workplaces, but for a small business, keeping up with the volume of regulations that are issued can be a real challenge. Trying to be compliant with every single new regulation would probably cost the average small business a prohibitively large amount of money. I recently visited a plant that utilized machines built in the late 1940s. They were high-quality machines that ran on belt-driven pulley systems. The guards around the pulleys, though, had gaps where fingers could potentially get caught. The pulleys were in the back of the machines, away from the area where employees worked, and it was obvious to all of the employees that they should keep their hands away from the gaps.

However, the owner was told by a safety auditor that these machines were not compliant with OSHA regulations and that if an OSHA inspector were to visit the facility, it would be cited for not having the machines properly protected. As a proactive measure, the owner attempted to resolve the issue. Several fabricators took a look at it, and the best estimate to retrofit a guard to each machine was about $3,500. Given that the machines cost less even when they were new, it seemed absurd to spend that much money. Unfortunately, small business owners frequently must choose between making expensive improvements that seem unnecessary and being at risk for being cited for an OSHA violation or, worse, having an employee injured on the job.

4. Our increasingly litigious society. Wrongful termination lawsuits, environmental protection issues, and other litigation have dramatically increased operating costs. These costs haven't risen just because of lawsuits but because of the protective and reactive paperwork required. Human resources departments have grown out of necessity to deal with all these issues, further adding to costs. Whatever your feelings about the validity of some of this litigation, odds are that it affects your small business, whether in the form of an actual or threatened lawsuit or an increase in your costs across the board.

5. Rising costs of supplies and suppliers. Whether you're a manufacturer or service provider, you've probably seen a steady rise in these costs in recent years. Material costs for manufacturers have risen progressively, and service companies are struggling with increases on everything from coffee to paper. The fees charged by accountants, public relations agencies, consultants, and other suppliers also continue to skyrocket.

6. The pace of technological advances. Many small businesses are focused on obtaining state-of-the-art, high-tech equipment. It seems that every year brings a technological sea change that makes the old computer hardware and software obsolete and necessitates the purchase of new systems. To a certain extent, these dramatic technological advances have been useful for small companies. It is sometimes difficult to know, however, when we're seduced by the bells and whistles rather than the real functionality of these devices. Nonetheless, we feel we need to keep buying new products—whether they are cell phones, monitors, or printers—and driving expenses higher.

7. Spiraling salaries. Partly because of union demands and partly because of the need for a better-educated, more specialized workforce, salaries have become an increasingly large cost for small businesses. It is very difficult to control salaries in small companies, especially in industries where employers compete for employees and talented people can almost name their price. Employees in the information technology sector, in particular, are negotiating for top salaries in even the smallest of companies.

If these seven factors don't motivate you to start controlling costs and spending more wisely, look at these issues from another perspective. Specifically, let's examine how many small companies run their businesses today and the mistakes they make that leave them no room for financial error.

WHY FISCALLY CONSERVATIVE SMALL BUSINESS HAS BECOME A THING OF THE PAST

Certainly some small companies exist that are fiscally conservative, but for a number of reasons, we're seeing a rise in small firms that either are financially aggressive or lack the system of checks and balances that used to be standard for small businesses. To an extent, small companies do have to be more aggressive than in the past if they want to remain competitive. They need to invest in a new cutting-edge material or make a greater commitment to marketing, or else they'll lose out to the big company that has recently moved into their marketplace or the Internet competitor that is marketing to their customers.

Unfortunately, many small companies have overreacted to competitive threats. In addition, some small business owners have become big-picture thinkers like their CEO counterparts at big corporations, excelling at strategy but taking their eyes off of financial controls.

In addition, I've witnessed many small business owners succumb to the "growth company" lure. They want to be known as aggressive, expansion-minded businesspeople, and they therefore take financial risks to become bigger. Because of e-commerce expansion possibilities and better access to venture capital money and lower interest rates (at least in recent years), the temptation to get bigger is powerful.

I'm not suggesting expansion is bad, only that expansionist tendencies can place small companies in hot water—hot water they were often able to avoid when they pursued more conservative business strategies.

Similarly, many small companies borrow too much, whether to fuel growth strategies or for other reasons. While loans are often necessary to fund plant modernization and other important improvements, too much debt can place companies in precarious financial straits. Borrowing less over a longer period is often a more fiscally responsible approach.

Not all of these mistakes may apply to you. I would bet, however, that at least one of them does and that you can see why it is even more imperative today than in the past to control costs. To ascertain just how important it is, let's see how these mistakes and trends apply to your company.

ASSESS HOW MUCH YOUR COMPANY NEEDS TO SAVE MONEY

The following checklist includes a wide range of events or situations that make a cost-saving strategy absolutely essential. Review the list and place a checkmark next to any item that applies to your company.

____ Foreign competition has eroded our market significantly.

____ During the past two years, we've had at least one major increase in our health care insurance costs.

____ To meet governmental safety requirements, we've had to spend over $10,000 in the last year.

___ We've been sued much more in the last five years (by a customer, employee, or other party) than in the previous ten years.

___ Our suppliers have increased their prices beyond what we feel is fair.

___ We regularly make expensive upgrades to our computer hardware and software.

___ We're involved in a war for talent and have therefore had to overpay to get top people.

___ We've grown too fast and have incurred significant costs as a result.

___ We have not done as good a job as we should have in keeping an eye on costs.

___ We've introduced new products and services that required significant investments.

___ Our main source of funding reduced the money they provided, or that funding source was eliminated entirely.

___ When our market changed, we had difficulty adapting to this change, and this failure cost us a lot of money.

If you found yourself making more than one or two checkmarks, recognize that you are a victim of trends and events that have impacted all types of small businesses; understand, too, that prevailing management styles and business strategies also made you vulnerable.

Now examine the following questions and see which ones you answer affirmatively.

___ Have you experienced a financial crisis in the last three years?

___ Was the crisis so severe that you had to lay off employees?

___ Has your company experienced a sudden loss of a major customer or a market shift that put you in precarious financial straits?

____ Has your organization found itself struggling because of money needed to defend itself against an employee discrimination lawsuit?

____ Has a governmental agency demanded that you make changes in your business or physical plant to avoid being in violation of laws or regulations?

____ Did you lose one or more key employees in the last year whose departure had a significant negative impact on your business?

____ Are you finding that your competitors are no longer limited to a handful of traditional companies in your industry but now include foreign competitors, divisions of large corporations, and Internet-based businesses?

____ In the past year, have you experienced a significant loss and regretted spending a sizeable amount of money on a new computer system, additional staff, or some other expense?

____ As your expenses for salaries, materials, safety, marketing, and other goods and services have risen, have you seen an offsetting rise in revenue?

____ Do you feel that your company still manages and spends money as if it were the boom years of the late 1990s?

Again, the more affirmative answers you have, the more your company needs to focus on controlling costs. Now let me provide you with a more positive reason for embarking on a savings plan.

OPPORTUNITY COSTS

As I've emphasized before, you're not being frugal for frugality's sake. Saving money is a means to an end—two ends, actually. The first offers you protection against setbacks and downturns. The second offers you additional funds to take advantage of opportunities.

More than in the past, opportunities are arising for small businesses in all industries. Specifically, following are some factors catalyzing these opportunities.

Internet access. The Internet has connected small companies to new markets, partners, and purchasing possibilities. In the past, many small manufacturers tended to buy replacement parts from local distributors or depend on a few long-time suppliers. Now any small company can go on the Internet and find replacement parts for less cost or in less time, or both. Similarly, I know a small market research firm in Cleveland whose clients were located primarily in that area. By aggressively joining various online communities of interest, they networked with enough people to establish relationships with companies throughout the United States. Eventually, this translated into clients located across a broader geographical area.

Big company outsourcing. Huge companies have caught the outsourcing bug, providing unprecedented opportunities for small companies that can take over functions (or parts of functions) that were formerly handled in-house. Small businesses that not too long ago would never have had a chance to work for IBM, General Motors, and other large companies are now enjoying these opportunities.

Volatility of customer-supplier relationships. A small business owner may well lament the passing of customer-supplier loyalty and the fact that relationships usually don't last 10 or 20 years as they did in the past. At the same time, the volatility of these relationships gives companies a chance to get in the door at customers that formerly locked out suppliers other than the one with which they had a longstanding relationship.

Boundary-crossing mentality. This factor is more psychological than anything else. It wasn't unusual for the head of a small company to say, "I'm not going to go after their business; they're too (big, far away, different culturally, demanding, etc.)." This mentality has changed. Small business owners, as well as prospective customers, don't have as many preconceived ideas about whom they'll work with. They recognize that in the new world of diversity and heterogeneity, the old boundaries don't apply.

Global markets. Again, this is both a positive and a negative development. As I've mentioned, the global world means that a competitor from China can come in and draw away your customers in Biloxi. At the same time, however, you may find that a great new market exists for your products or services in China—and that company in China is much more receptive to your pitch than it was in the past.

The need for flexibility and speed. Many small companies by nature possess these traits, which are prized by customers who are tired of the bureaucratic red tape and rigid procedures of larger suppliers. Nimble small businesses can reap all sorts of dividends because of their ability to adjust to circumstance and meet tight deadlines.

These opportunities require money to pursue. You need to spend more on marketing to go after global customers, you must invest more in a good Web site to capitalize on the Internet, and you must provide your salespeople with a larger budget to go after accounts that are more spread out geographically.

If you can save some money through a well-thought-out plan, you can direct these saved dollars toward emerging opportunities. You'll recall that I mentioned our company saved $8,400 one year by reducing a phone bill. When we heard about a great deal on computer monitors—the type of deal that has become much more common in our economy—we were able to spend a good portion of that $8,400 savings on new monitors for everyone in our office.

The purchase improved both morale and performance, but we probably would have been reluctant to make this purchase without our phone savings.

THE COMFORT OF A CUSHION

Perhaps the most compelling reason to adopt a savvy cost-saving policy today is the need for a cushion. I don't think I'm being alarmist when I write that for many small companies, bankruptcy is just one lost customer or one crisis away. Nonetheless, I know of many small companies that operate on the financial edge. There are companies that finance some of their debt through banks—which is fine—but they must meet financial ratios related to performance that leave little margin for error. One bad quarter could mean that the bank owns their company. Similarly, I know small business owners who are content to run companies that just manage to break even each year, and as long as they can pay their salary and those of their employees, they believe everything is fine.

They should be aware of Murphy's Law: anything that can go wrong will go wrong. It strikes me as foolhardy to run a business today with no financial margin for error or crisis. Small business owners should do everything possible to give themselves a bit of a cushion, and one of the best ways of doing so is by cutting unnecessary costs. This cushion isn't a panacea, but it can buy you just enough time to get through a downturn and be ready and able to take advantage of the upturn when it arrives.

Of course, every small business owner probably defines a cushion differently. For one company, having $5,000 or $10,000 in additional funds may be sufficient. For another company, the sum has to be larger to get through an emergency situation.

That's the great thing about creating a small business savings plan. As you'll discover, you can choose to be aggressive in your plan and build a large cushion or be conservative and build the cushion gradually. In the next chapter, I'll show you one way to start building that protective cushion by employing a recession mentality.

THE RECESSION TEST AND OTHER CONSCIOUSNESS- RAISING TOOLS

One of the biggest challenges for small business owners is raising their consciousness when it comes to saving and spending. This is especially true if they haven't been in business a long time or have not suffered any major downturns. Some business owners who have suffered downturns, though, also have selective memories; they tell themselves that their one bad year was an anomaly and that the forces that caused it are unlikely to reoccur. All of these individuals also possess an entrepreneurial optimism that precludes looking at the worst-case possibilities.

I'm all for entrepreneurial optimism. Without it, not many people would start or stick with small businesses in today's challenging environment. What I'm suggesting is that this optimism operate hand in hand with a probing, financially aware mindset. Cost consciousness is not about being pessimistic or always believing bankruptcy is around the corner. Instead, it means being vigilant for opportunities to reduce costs or spend more wisely.

Vigilance is difficult to maintain, not only because of the optimistic mind-set of many small business owners but also because of the daily demands of running a business. Caught up in their stressful routines, people forget to assess all the ways they might save money. They may temporarily become aware of costs when they're presented with a bill they think is unusually high or when business is bad, but most of the time, they don't invest much time or energy in cost-conscious thinking.

The recession test helps foster this thinking. As you'll see, it's an easy-to-use tool that focuses your attention on cost reduction and smart spending. Let's start out by understanding how you can apply this test to your business and how it can change the way you think about saving and spending.

WHAT IF A RECESSION WERE TO HIT TOMORROW?

This question may be one you don't normally ask yourself. Even if you're convinced no recession is in sight, I'd like you to suspend your disbelief for a moment and consider the question. More specifically, ask yourself the following questions:

> *If the economy tanked and tomorrow I knew that we had to cut at least $100,000 in expenses or go under, where might I find reductions to equal this amount of money?*

> *What if my sales were to drop by 20 or 30 percent tomorrow? Could we survive? Where would we have to make cuts in our business to remain profitable?*

With these questions in mind, here are a series of additional questions that will determine if you can pass the recession test:

1. Are there any unproductive or marginally productive employees who might be let go without any negative effect?

2. Are there employees who are marginally or moderately productive who can be retrained and become more productive?

3. Are there luxuries that your company has enjoyed in good times—free health club memberships for employees, an expensive office lease—that you could do without if you had to?

4. Do you ever analyze what you might sell—a division, equipment, intellectual property—that would generate dollars without hurting the business?

5. During the past year, do you recall looking over the budget or an invoice and saying to yourself (or someone else), "We're really spending a lot on X"?

6. Do you neglect to review your employee benefits plans regularly and analyze ways in which you could be providing essentially the same major benefits for less cost?

7. Are you reluctant to place spending limits on nonessential (to the core business) items—office supplies, holiday party— and do you rationalize how these costs seem to rise annually?

8. When you buy products or services from a supplier, do you usually refrain from trying to negotiate a lower price?

It's likely that most of you answered yes to some or even all of these questions. What you should be doing is asking yourself these questions consistently and doing something about at least some of them. The recession test is a test of whether you act on the cost-cutting possibilities before an economic downturn hits. Do you make the effort to analyze whether a given action should be undertaken right now, and if so, are you willing to do something about it?

The recession test, then, is nothing more than being consistently aware of these eight questions and determining:

- If I were to take the action suggested right now, what would be better and what would be worse in my business?

- Does the better outweigh the worse, not just in terms of dollars but from the perspective of the business's reputation, morale of employees, and process efficiency and effectiveness?

Now I'd like to share with you how this test evolved, since its origins demonstrate why I believe it's so valuable. During the last recession, our business was struggling, and we needed to cut operating costs. Like many small companies, we looked first at salaries and ranked every individual in the company from biggest contributor on down. One individual became the obvious choice. We had to make a number of tough cost-cutting decisions, and one of them was to lay off this employee. It turned out it was the right decision for the business. Other people in this person's department had to take up the slack, since we didn't hire someone to replace him, but very quickly, things were running more effectively than before he left. With everyone pitching in and some changes to the work process in this department, things worked perfectly.

After this experience, I thought about why I had not fired this individual five years before, when I realized he wasn't pulling his weight, he was unhappy with his job, and we really didn't need him. Part of the problem was that I felt loyalty to him, since he was a long-time employee. Part of the problem was that I, like many small business owners, secretly believe that every employee is indispensable and that the sky will come crashing down if that person is gone.

Then I did some calculations. If we had eliminated this person five years ago, we would have saved at least $150,000 in salary and benefits!

I'm not suggesting that you fire people left and right in a quest to reduce costs. What I am asking you to do is imagine yourself in the middle of a recession and picture the actions you would take to survive that downturn. Thinking about these actions, ask yourself: How much better off would we be if we had taken these cost-cutting steps five years ago, rather than waiting for the recession to force our hand?

COMPARISON SHOP

When you're in the market for a new car, you probably don't buy the first one you see and willingly pay the listed price. Most people shop around and negotiate before making the purchase. With a recession mind-set, you also don't accept costs as immutable. Instead, you routinely question what you're paying for everything. This doesn't mean spending all your time trying to save a nickel or always questioning your employees about why they paid a certain amount for a given product or service. Instead, you simply make it a habit to comparison shop.

For instance, we hired a new employee who was in charge of purchasing office supplies. Like many small companies, we had fallen into a routine of ordering the same supplies from the same suppliers, but this new person came from a different company with a different approach. Therefore, one of the first things she did was find a catalog she used in her previous job and compare the prices of various products with those offered by our current supplier. She discovered that the catalog offered considerable savings on a number of items, and she used these facts to negotiate a much better deal—15 percent off what we were paying, saving us about $1,500 annually. Plus, she negotiated a next-day delivery clause into the deal.

Cost-conscious business owners comparison shop in a different way. When I meet with other small business CEOs at conferences or other forums, we will be talking about the purchase of a new piece of equipment or obtaining a new lease or retooling a plant, and one savvy individual will ask, "How much did you pay for that?" Of course, your particular purchase and another company's may involve different factors that affect price, but in many instances, the comparative question yields valuable information. You may discover a great new supplier who can save you a lot of money. You may also discover a buying approach that helps you control costs.

I should add that some business owners pay no attention whatsoever to these discussions; to them, it's like comparing apples and oranges. They believe another business owner in another industry in another location couldn't possibly know anything that would benefit their own businesses. In some instances, perhaps that's true. Many times, though, a tip or technique is universally applicable. Someone may tell you of an Internet site that offers great deals on a particular piece of machinery or suggest a technique to cut all your printing costs. Whatever it is, you need to be conscious of these cost-saving ideas, or they'll go right by you.

To help foster this consciousness, ask yourself the following questions regularly when you receive an invoice, are contemplating making a major purchase, or are reviewing suppliers:

- Based on my gut reaction, does this price seem fair?
- Have I ever explored alternatives to this supplier or purchase price?
- For how long have I been buying from this supplier at roughly the same terms: a few months or less, close to a year, a few years, more than five years?
- Have I recently spoken to someone at another company with the same title as I have about how much they pay for this item?
- Would this be a good opportunity to explore alternative sources, such as Internet sites, catalogs, and foreign suppliers?
- Is it possible that I can get this product or service for less if I try to negotiate based on volume, a longstanding relationship, or another factor?

CREATE WORST-CASE SCENARIOS

The following exercise is not a contradiction of what I noted earlier. I don't want you to go around like Chicken Little, worried that the sky is falling. Or to quote another adage, financially paranoid small business executives are penny wise and pound foolish. This exercise is designed to consider calamities and catastrophes that are unlikely to happen but will push you and your employees to be more recession-minded in regard to saving and spending. I've found that if you can imagine the worst happening, you can operate with an awareness of what it would take for these events to drag your company under. Therefore, consider the following scenarios.

Your biggest customer suddenly drops you. What would you do if your biggest customer or client deserted you? What actions might you take if this unfortunate event transpired? Make a list of specific things you would do, from reducing staff to placing a lid on expenses to reconfiguring your budget to spend more money on finding new customers. Note specific steps that would help you both survive in the short run and reach your longer-term goals.

Inflation spirals out of control. Create a list of options for this economic scenario. How might it impact the money you're paying for your lease, rental agreements, salaries, bonuses, and supplies? What specific steps can you take to hold costs down? Might you bring certain tasks in-house that you formerly farmed out? Might you change your corporate investment strategy or how benefit monies are invested?

A major lawsuit is filed against you. Suddenly your legal costs are skyrocketing because of an employee discrimination lawsuit or a government lawsuit naming you as a polluter. You need to apportion a sizable amount of money to fight the lawsuit, requiring you to make cuts in other areas. Create a list of areas where you can immediately reduce your spending without doing serious harm to the business. For each item on the list, estimate the dollars you might save and the potential negative results of the reduction. Then prioritize each item on the list in terms of these two factors (i.e., the item with biggest amount saved and the least harm would be the number one priority).

Once you've completed this exercise, you'll have a number of action items. Some of them you might never want to put into effect unless one of these worst-case scenarios occurs. Others, however, can be implemented sooner rather than later without any negative repercussions. At the very least, you can keep these actions in mind and take advantage of them when the time seems right.

THE WRONG THINGS TO DO

As you attempt to develop cost consciousness, you need to be cautious not to go overboard. When I've spoken about this subject in front of groups, often someone misinterprets what I'm saying and assumes that the message is to save as much as you can as quick as you can. I cannot overemphasize that slashing budgets and cutting staff has consequences. In your desire to reduce costs, you may also lose a key person who can make your business a great deal of money or fail to maintain a piece of equipment that breaks down and costs the company a mint. To help you avoid these negative repercussions, following is a list of common mistakes small business owners make.

Reduce advertising and sales budgets in anticipation of a drop in business. Perhaps you foresee a decline in sales because of a new competitor's success or because of a general economic slump. Whatever the cause, you decide that the easiest budget cut to make is in marketing, since it doesn't affect your core business. You assume that you can restore the cuts when business improves.

In most instances, however, if your volume drops, the last thing you want to do is reduce advertising and sales expenditures. The ads that don't run or the tools the sales force lacks may cause you to miss an opportunity that you otherwise would have capitalized on. When times get tough, you want to maintain your presence in the marketplace. Certainly if there is an unproductive salesperson, it may make sense to eliminate that position, but you should save these cuts for real emergencies rather than using them as preventative measures.

Nitpick about expenditures. Being aware of costs and saving opportunities is very different from micromanaging every expenditure. The last thing your company needs is for you to be devoting most of your time to saving pennies. If you're the top person or one of the top people in your small company, your example will make everyone paranoid about spending anything. Your sudden obsession with money will make other people overly wary of even minor costs. A salesperson may not take a customer out to lunch for fear that you're going to get upset when you see the expense report. Your MIS manager may not upgrade the computer system for fear you'll view it as an unnecessary expense.

Here's a cautionary tale from the owner of a small public relations agency. This individual, whom we'll call Bill, started his agency about 20 years ago, and during that first year or two, he admits he was a "maniac" about costs. Things were tight, and he was certain that if he didn't account for every penny, his agency would fold. He would check every shipping, phone, and utility bill himself, and if any expense seemed out of line, he would confront whoever was responsible for what Bill deemed excessive spending. Bill said it got to the point that his seven-person staff was terrified to spend a penny without his approval, and so his people developed the unofficial policy of marching into his office four or five times a day to get his approval on purchases of pencils, paper, and other minor expenditures. At first, Bill was pleased that his staff was seeking approvals before spending, but one day when he came home from work, his wife asked him what he'd done that day. Bill told her, and she said, "You know, every time I ask you about your day, you talk about how you debated with Steve about whether he should pay an additional $10 for overnight delivery versus two-day delivery or how you and your office manager went from one store to the next until you found a discount on printer cartridges. You're always complaining to me that the business isn't as profitable as it should be, but you and your people aren't going to come up with the big ideas to make it profitable unless you stop wasting time on nickel-and-dime stuff." Chastised by his wife's speech, Bill stopped nitpicking expenses.

A much more effective approach is to be selective and discrete in your approach to spending. Don't yell and lecture when someone overspends; have a quiet one-on-one discussion about the importance of watching costs. Don't demand to see every invoice every day in every department. Instead, be vigilant about spending—but don't be overbearing or obsessive.

Keep your concerns about overspending to yourself. While you should be careful not to nitpick about spending, it's still important to be open and communicative about the financial culture of your small business. If you're worried about the direction the business is going and have legitimate concerns about problems your company is facing, the worst thing you can do is keep everything to yourself and then suddenly announce that you have to cut staff by 15 percent. This might be standard procedure in a larger company, but in a small company, this "surprise" will feel like a betrayal. In leadership development circles, *transparency* has become a big word. It means that leaders should be sufficiently open about both their hopes and fears that they foster a sense of inclusiveness among their people.

Therefore, aim to be transparent, at least to some extent. Share your concerns that you might have to cut staff if sales don't improve in the next year. Communicate that you're worried about rising prices for raw materials and that some changes may need to be made if prices continue to rise. In this way, if you have to reduce spending and especially staff, people won't be devastated by the cuts. They may not be happy about them, but they will understand why they were necessary.

Lori, the head of a catalog company, holds regular financial meetings with her nonfinancial managers. She calls them "state of the business" discussions, and she uses them both to communicate significant financial challenges or advantages facing the business and to answer her employees' questions about these issues. Lori said that before she started holding these meetings, rumors spread quickly among her 80 employees whenever a problem surfaced. At one point, a top executive left the company abruptly, and everyone assumed it meant that he was aware of a serious financial problem and had left the ship before it sank. In reality, the executive was simply burned out and wanted to take a year off. Lori learned that if she kept managerial staff abreast of the company's financial status, rumors were nipped in the bud. She also found that even when the company was facing a financial challenge, talking about it openly helped to avoid the panicky response that rumors often produced.

This transparency is also an effective way to instill cost consciousness in other people. By addressing legitimate concerns about spending with a range of people in the company, you raise their awareness of major cost issues in the business. Some small business owners are reluctant to do this because they worry that people will start looking for other jobs if they get the impression that the business is in trouble. I've found that this is unlikely to happen if you don't adopt a doom-and-gloom attitude or turn minor cost problems into major ones. It really is just a question of sharing key pieces of information with your staff, so that they know you're focused on controlling costs and they adopt a similar focus.

WHY PERSONNEL CUTS AND A PEOPLE-FIRST PHILOSOPHY AREN'T MUTUALLY EXCLUSIVE

Many small business people work hard to create a "family atmosphere," and they come to think of their employees as family. As a result, it's difficult to kick a son or daughter out of the house. Yet under certain circumstances, you have no alternative. In the life of most small companies, there comes a time when you need to cut staff out of financial necessity. Maybe you have to let only a few people go, or maybe you must reduce staff by a larger percentage. If you're not prepared for this eventuality, you may end up letting the wrong people go. If you're not aware of how much each person contributes to or detracts from your overall business, you may not know whom to let go and make a choice based simply on seniority or titles.

As unpleasant a task as it may be, the recession-minded CEO creates a list of all employees and ranks them in order of value to the company. In this way, if the time comes when letting people go is a financial necessity, those who contribute the least will be the first to go. Implementing staff cuts is difficult, but if you have to do it, you should be fair about it. I've found that the remaining employees are better able to adjust to downsizing if they believe that the right people were let go.

To determine who the right people are, give each employee a point for the following attributes:

- Contributes ideas and innovations that help the company run profitably and grow
- Uses skills to make sure jobs get done effectively and on time
- Has knowledge that would be difficult for the company to replace
- Displays managerial or leadership qualities that bring out the best in others

- Possesses a good attitude that makes this person valuable on teams and for morale
- Has been a loyal, productive employee for a significant period of time
- Embodies values that make the company what it is

Subtract a point for any of the following:

- Creates dissension and poor morale among other employees
- Arrives late for work and leaves early regularly
- Complains frequently about assignments, environment, or other factors
- Sabotages projects through indifference or from not seeing the necessity of the assignment
- Goes about the job without enthusiasm or creativity

If someone is especially strong in any of the first areas, or especially weak in the second, double the points you give to or subtract from that individual.

The goal here isn't to determine who your top people are but who is least valuable. Admittedly, this is a subjective process, but it should provide at least some sense of whom you can let go with the least harm to the company.

IDENTIFY THE BIG-TICKET ITEMS

To develop a cost-conscious mentality, you need to be aware of all the areas in which you can potentially reduce expenditures. It's surprising that many small company bosses have only a vague idea about which items or areas are costing the company the most. As a result, they may focus all their time and attention on reducing the company phone bill, but in reality, that bill is a middling company expenditure rather than a major expense.

The financially savvy CEO, on the other hand, is aware of the high-ticket spending categories within the company and is continuously thinking about and experimenting with ways to reduce these costs. The CEO may not always be successful in this regard but is always thinking about what expenses would have to be cut if things went south.

To create a similar awareness of big-ticket expenditures in your company, do the following:

- Obtain an accounts payable report and sort it from the highest dollar value to the lowest. Make this report public. Let everyone know where the money is going. In most companies, the biggest category expenditure is salaries. While many people may realize this, they may not know that the second largest category expenditure is computer equipment, or advertising, or raw materials. Similarly, you and your top people may assume that a particular type of purchase is high on the list, when actually it's in the middle or in the lower half. Too often, companies keep this information secret. I'm not suggesting you should publish everyone's individual salaries or even break it down by departments, but publishing this information once or twice a year will do a good job of making people cost conscious and aware of where the company's major expenditures lie.

- Analyze where you might make feasible cuts in five or ten of the big-ticket categories. By feasible cuts, I mean reductions that are realistic given the needs of your business. Yes, you might save a great deal of money if you cut staff by 50 percent, but you would be unable to do the work and would quickly go out of business. On the other hand, if the company spent $2 million on materials over the course of a year, and you determined that you might save at least 1 percent on your materials costs through negotiation with current suppliers and finding new suppliers, you would realize an annual savings of $20,000. This recognition might be enough to motivate you to do something about it.

- Look at specific big-ticket invoices and ask "what if" and "how" questions. In other words, as you're reviewing invoices involving outside professional services (such as advertising agencies, public relations agencies, or consultants), ask, "What if we reduced our budget for professional services by 3 percent; would there be any significant negative consequences? How would we go about this reduction in the most effective manner possible?" Again, this questioning doesn't mean that you will take a specific action, only that you're making yourself aware of it as a possibility. Maintaining a broad awareness of potential savings is part of the consciousness-raising process.

GOOD TIMES, BAD HABITS

Almost every small business owner I interviewed noted that it was especially difficult to maintain spending and saving awareness during good economic times. When profits are up, the economy is healthy, and the company's strategy appears sound, small business CEOs tend to be free with their spending. As one individual told me, "If I don't make that major new investment in equipment now, when am I going to make it?"

Spending on necessary improvements or new initiatives makes perfect sense when cash is rolling in. At the same time, however, you can be vigilant about spending even as you're writing the checks. This may seem like a paradox, but you can manage spending effectively if you remind yourself that the profits and the rosy outlook that allow you to spend now won't exist in a matter of months . . . or perhaps weeks!

One of the company CEOs I interviewed has adapted a Japanese business practice to keep his eye trained on saving money even in the best of times. As part of his business improvement process, he asks the question "Why?" five times to find the root cause of a problem or its solution. Therefore, when someone presents him with a proposal to purchase new software for the company, suggests that they increase the sales department's travel budget, or insists that they must move to a larger facility, this CEO asks questions such as: "Why do we need a larger facility? Why will the facility we're considering purchasing meet our needs better than the one we have? Why don't we examine the pros and cons of adding on to our current facility?"

Finally, and perhaps most importantly, you should communicate that cutting costs and spending wisely are positive rather than negative actions. During good times, especially, no one wants to come across as being risk-averse or a pessimist. People are reluctant to raise their hands and question expenditures, even when their instinct or their knowledge tells them that something is a waste of money. Small business owners must communicate a positive attitude about frugality regularly. Following are some ways our company and other small business owners do so.

Keep a dialog going about cost-saving innovations. This especially includes those that are implemented. This dialog can be informal chats between department heads and their employees about who suggested what and how it helped the company save money. Some companies have a more formal approach, issuing memos or reporting the savings method in a newsletter. Still others send e-mails to everyone in the company about a creative approach. Whatever method you choose, try to make this an ongoing dialog that becomes part of the culture rather than a one-time discussion.

Reward individuals who come up with significant spending or saving ideas. One of the companies I talked to has made this a major competency that is assessed during performance reviews.

Every manager in this organization knows that finding ways to be cost conscious is expected and fosters this behavior in the employees. At our company, bonuses are tied to cost-saving programs and plans. Just the other day, my purchasing manager told me that our grinding wheel supplier had made a mistake and some wheels were too small in diameter. Normally, we reject wheels that are too large or too small (it is not an uncommon problem), even though it doesn't affect functionality and results in only a 5 or 10 percent loss in the wheel's life. Our purchasing manager, though, decided to negotiate with the supplier for a better price on the wheels that were slightly irregular and ended up buying a batch of $78 wheels for $50, resulting in a $600 savings.

Use the sawmill metaphor. Bend over backward to communicate that you don't want people to be cheap and that you really do get what you pay for. You're going to need to reiterate this point, since some people always think that being cost conscious means squeezing every penny that crosses their path. A more apt way to explain the goal of cost consciousness is by explaining your philosophy of getting the most out of what you have and what you spend.

The sawmill metaphor conveys this concept nicely. Sawmills try to get the most out of every log they cut because raw material costs are one of their biggest expenses. They try to optimize the number of board feet of lumber from every log and minimize the amount of sawdust and trim waste. To this purpose, they scan each log before cutting to figure out how they can obtain the most board feet from the log. They position the log exactly the right way and use the thinnest saw blades available to help achieve this goal. They then use the sawdust and wood chips produced by the cutting as fuel for the kilns that dry the lumber. Nothing is left to waste, but they use top materials and produce a top-quality product. This is exactly the philosophy that helps create cost-conscious but not cheap employees.

3

ARE EMPLOYEE BENEFITS BENEFITING YOU?

Many small business owners view employee benefits as a problem rather than an opportunity. More specifically, they see this area as a rising cost over which they have little control. They bemoan how their health insurance premiums continue to skyrocket and how all their other plans continue to increase in cost. They complain that there's little they can do about these expenses and that only big companies are in a position to manage these costs effectively.

While I'd be the last person to tell you that providing employees with some form of health insurance isn't costly, I would also advise you that many options exist for controlling these and other benefit plan costs. Based on my interviews with other small business owners and my own experiences in this area, I know that as long as you're open-minded and creative, you can reduce this particular expense. More importantly, you can reconfigure your benefits not only to save money over what you're currently paying but also to create the right mix of benefits for your employees.

Too often, small business owners get locked into standard benefit plans and refuse to explore other ways of offering benefits. In fact, I've known a number of small company CEOs who knew next to nothing about their employee benefits, preferring to assign this task to their human resources or administrative staff. However, if you want to control your costs, you need to possess a certain amount of knowledge, starting with what plans are costing you the most money.

RANKING YOUR COSTS

Off the top of your head, do you know what percentage your health insurance costs represent in relation to total benefit plan expenditures? Here is a typical breakdown of the five most common plan costs, based on my informal survey of other small business owners:

1. Health insurance	75.0%
2. 401(k)/pension/profit sharing	10.0%
3. Life insurance	5.0%
4. Dental insurance	5.0%
5. Holiday parties	1.5%

Some small business presidents are aghast at how much they are spending on health insurance, and they decide to eliminate this benefit. I would not recommend this option if at all possible for both humanistic and business reasons. Companies that eliminate health coverage suffer from unhealthy employee attitudes, especially if their workers have enjoyed a good benefit plan for years. They see this cut as the beginning of the end and quickly begin looking for other jobs, develop poor morale, and show reduced productivity. In fact, reducing health insurance coverage to bare bones is also a bad idea, in that it produces a similarly negative effect.

A much better approach is to consider the percentages listed and determine if they are in line with your percentages. If, for instance, you are spending only 50 percent on health insurance and 25 percent on the 401(k) category, then your spending is probably out of whack. If you are investing a disproportionate amount of money in parties, life insurance, and dental coverage, then you are probably fooling yourself into believing that employees will accept the trade-off of good teeth for an extensive PPO network. Health insurance averages 75 percent of total benefits spending for a reason. In fact, it may be the number one reason employees apply for jobs at your company and stay there. When you think about health insurance as a recruiting tool, as a morale builder, and a way to keep key employees, then the expense is much more palatable. Therefore, unless you have some compelling reason for not falling in line with these percentages, you should make changes that allow you to do so.

Second, don't assume that you're paying the going rate for health insurance and that there are no deals to be had. I've found that this assumption is not always valid and that insurance agents sometimes take advantage of naïve small business owners. At the very least, talk to other small companies in your area and ask what they're paying for their health insurance plans. An organization we belong to called the Employers Resource Association (ERA), for instance, provides results of a survey about what other small companies are paying for health insurance. No doubt, you can find similar information by contacting your industry trade group or another small business association in your geographic area. As when you are dealing with any supplier, you want to explore your options. These options are critical for companies that want to manage their health care costs instead of being managed by them, as the following section describes.

SEVEN WAYS TO REDUCE YOUR HEALTH CARE COSTS

Here are seven tactics that our company and others have used successfully. While none of them is a panacea for rising health care premiums, they all can provide significant relief for companies struggling to keep up with these rising premiums. Consider implementing one or more of the following approaches.

1. Talk to a local insurance broker. A number of small business owners I surveyed negotiate their deals directly with insurance companies. Brokers often are able to negotiate better rates than business owners can, so it would be wise to talk to someone who may secure a better rate or can at least offer you some suggestions for finding a lower-cost plan that better suits your particular situation.

2. Offer employees incentives for deferring coverage. The odds are that at least some of your employees will take you up on this offer. Married employees may have spouses who receive good insurance coverage from their companies, for example. Employees in their 20s may be able to obtain less expensive coverage on their own or through groups to which they belong. A 25-year-old person in good health can often obtain relatively low-cost coverage with high deductibles because of being in the low-risk category. Recognize, too, that some of your married employees had separate policies before they got married and maintained these policies without giving them much thought. In other instances, people feel more comfortable being insured through their employer rather than through a spouse's company; they have a certain amount of trust in being insured by their own companies. Consider how it might work if you were to offer your employees an incentive to defer coverage. As of this writing, it costs a small company about $10,000 annually to provide an individual with health insurance. If you offer that employee a $2,000 bonus for declining the company's medical coverage, you save about $8,000! Many times, an employee is eligible for coverage through a larger company, school, or governmental agency that offers a more comprehensive plan. Be aware, however, that some insurance companies have restrictions on spousal coverage; they won't allow employees who already have coverage with their own employers to be covered through their spouses. Similarly, some employers have tightened up restrictions on their policies, preventing nonemployee spouses from gaining coverage if they have the option of coverage from their own employer. Still, you may be one of the lucky ones who can take advantage of this option, so at least explore the possibility.

3. Stop offering insurance to retired employees. This offer is part of the culture in some small companies due to the caring, family-type environment they have established. It is a very nice benefit to make available for retired employees. Unfortunately, it is also a benefit that is no longer practical. If you are providing insurance for a significant number of older, retired employees, you also are probably paying an inflated insurance rate. People who are at or above retirement age drive up rates more than any other group—they're the ones who get sick most often and most seriously. Again, this tactic isn't about being callous. Retired employees have other insurance options such as Medicare and Medicaid, depending on their age. In fact, they are probably paying a high rate if you are allowing them to maintain their insurance after COBRA has expired. If your human resources department can assist retiring employees by explaining what insurance options are available to them, this may be even more of a benefit than allowing them to maintain insurance at a high rate. In addition, maintaining coverage for retired employees ends up punishing current employees. As rates rise, you will be forced to pass on some of the costs to current employees or even cancel coverage altogether.

Fritz Hoffmann, on the other hand, chose to stop covering his retired employees. He owns a company called Lunar Mold and Tool, and a number of his retired employees who were eligible for Medicare or Medicaid continued to receive coverage. This resulted in much higher rates for his other employees, and his health care provider informed him that if he were to drop these retirees from coverage, his rates would drop 16 percent. Fritz had no choice but to drop them, especially in a year when the average increase was around 13 percent—a 29 percent increase would have been intolerable. Fritz, like other humanistic small business owners, faced a tough decision. He wanted to reward loyal employees with postretirement health insurance coverage. Unfortunately, this reward is financially unfeasible in this day and age, especially for older companies who have hundreds or even thousands of retired employees.

4. Evaluate the viability of working through an employee leasing company. These leasing companies essentially take over all HR and administrative functions, including health insurance. Later, I'll address the pros and cons of employee leasing companies for small businesses in more detail, but for now, let me emphasize that they can reduce insurance rates significantly because your employees, along with the employees of other small companies, essentially become employed by the leasing company. As part of a larger group, you are often able to secure lower rates. I've found this is an especially attractive option for companies with 20 or fewer employees. For companies with more than 20 employees, it may not be as advantageous. Still, try to contact at least two employee leasing companies, provide them with the information they request, and secure quotes to get a sense of whether this option might help you to reduce your administrative and benefits expenditures.

5. Help your employees reduce their claims. Obviously, there's nothing you can do when your employees have real illnesses and need to access the health care system. If you and they are unlucky and they have expensive illnesses, your insurance company is going to increase your premiums correspondingly. At the same time, employees may be using their health care benefits in a variety of ways that result in higher costs for you. For instance, some people use emergency rooms as if they were doctor's offices, stopping in when they have minor ailments such as colds. Higher deductibles and copays make people think twice about using the system in this way. Of course, you don't want to set deductibles so high that people are discouraged from going to the doctor because of the cost. At the same time, the days of the $50 deductible are over, at least for most small companies.

In addition, you should do everything possible to encourage a healthy workforce. You have many ways to help your employees practice good health habits, such as offering incentives for people to quit smoking, sponsoring weight loss programs, or offering discounts for health club memberships. The more physically fit employees you have who eat healthy diets, who are physically active, and who don't smoke or drink to excess, the lower your health care costs are likely to be.

6. Establish Health Care Savings Accounts (HSAs). If you don't know about HSAs or have assumed they are not right for your company, you may want to learn about them or investigate them further. Approved by the U.S. government in December 2003, these plans have very high deductibles—some people refer to them as catastrophic health insurance coverage. Typically, deductibles are from $1,000 to $2,000 with annual caps on health care expenses at $5,000 to $10,000. With high-deductible plans, companies pay less for their employee health care insurance. Companies that have high-deductible plans are then able to fund HSAs for employees. These plans allow employees to set aside pretax dollars for medical and long-term care purposes. Money that is put into an HSA can be invested in an interest-earning account, carried forward year to year, and transferred to a new employer if the employee leaves the company.

If you choose to offer this type of plan to employees, be aware that you may encounter some initial resistance, especially when employees hear about the high deductibles. It will require some education to help them understand that the company will help reduce the deductible to a manageable level and that employees will receive all sorts of other benefits that can, in certain circumstances, be more advantageous to them than a traditional plan.

7. Offer Health Care Refund Accounts (HRAs). Similar to HSAs, these plans also come with high deductibles that companies reduce through funding. As the name implies, though, the funding takes place through a reimbursement program. Employees present their medical bills to employers and are reimbursed for their expenses up to a set amount.

If you're trying to decide whether an HSA or HRA best suits your company, consider the following example. Company X, with 50 employees, is willing to fund a $1,000 deductible for employees. With an HSA plan, Company X must set up accounts for all 50 employees and fund each account with $1,000. In other words, the company is immediately "out" $50,000—the accounts and the money in them are the employees'.

Company Y, on the other hand, wants to adopt an HRA with the same $1,000 deductible. They don't need to fund and set up $1,000 accounts for each employee. Instead, the company keeps track of how much of the $1,000 allowable each employee spends (to make sure employees don't exceed this amount) and reimburses expenditures.

Here is a key fact about HRAs: companies typically reimburse around 67 percent of employee expenditures annually. In other words, the average company is out only $33,500 rather than $50,000. Given that insurance companies charge the same for the high-deductible plan behind the HRA or HSA, the HRA seems to offer a significant savings advantage. I suggest talking with an insurance broker about the different ways an HRA plan can be designed and the pros and cons of both types of plans to see which might best fit your needs.

A SHORT-TERM WAY TO SHARE PROFITS

Most small business owners I've talked to have moved away from profit-sharing plans, not only because of their cost but because they have no motivational value, especially for younger employees. Try to convince a 30-year-old to work hard because if the company does well, employees will reap the benefits through profit sharing. Of course, an employee may appear to be appreciative, which convinces owners they should maintain their profit-sharing plans, but what the employee is really thinking is, "Oh boy! If I do a good job now and keep my nose to the grindstone, I'll receive a nice profit-sharing check in December. And I can't spend the money until I retire in 35 years!"

A much better alternative is gainsharing. As the name implies, this program rewards employees for above-average company performance. Most plans set performance goals on a monthly or quarterly basis, and if they're met, employees share in the wealth. We've been using gainsharing for seven years, and there have been times when employees have received payouts of almost an extra week's pay. Essentially, you're saying to these employees: "If you work hard enough and ship enough product while holding our costs down this month, I'll give you an extra week's pay."

This is a win-win from both savings and spending perspectives. Whatever gainsharing costs you incur, you receive incalculable benefits in terms of retention of key employees and higher morale.

I should add that gainsharing isn't for everyone. For one thing, it requires work and commitment from management; they must be able to capture costs accurately to track weekly performance. For another, it requires an owner who sees the long-term benefit and is willing to take a leap of faith. For a gainsharing plan to be successful, the reward for exceeding the established targets must be paid out immediately: immediate gratification drives positive employee behavior.

So let's say you get to the end of the first month of a gainsharing period, and $15,000 resides in the gainsharing pool. You contact the accounting department and tell them to distribute the money to everyone. In the second month, let's say you are at negative $15,000. The first thing that runs through the owner's or manager's mind is, "I just paid these guys $15,000 last month, and this month we are down $15,000; how is this helping me?" You should expect months when no payout occurs, and employees as well as owners and managers are perturbed that their hard work hasn't translated into additional money.

If you're interested in gainsharing, make sure you've thought about these and other financial scenarios. You need to set up the program so that you aren't paying money out to employees when you hit a gainsharing target but have not yet met your bottom-line, net profit goals. It may be that you should hire a gainsharing consultant to help you set up the program to meet your specific needs. To learn more, go to *www.gainsharinginc.com*.

Other viable profit-sharing options exist. I know one small company that shares a percentage of sales exceeding a designated level with employees. Another small business shares 3 percent of all sales dollars shipped in a given month. A publicly traded company awards shares of stock quarterly to employees if they hit key financial objectives. These and other profit-sharing programs often motivate employees to perform at high levels.

401(K) IS OKAY

Many small businesses have replaced their profit-sharing plans with 401(k)s, and for good reason. For instance, let's say you have had a profit-sharing plan for the last five years and employ 30 people. Let's assume you've shared $750 per employee on average over this five-year period, which comes out to $40,000 annually. Now take that amount and divide it by the average annual pay rate for your employees (let's further assume that your average salary is $30,000 per year). Therefore, $750 divided by $30,000 equals 2.5 percent. Rather than using a profit-sharing model, this 2.5 percent is the amount you could use to match at 100 percent what each employee puts into their 401(k).

Another way to think about it is matching 50 percent on the first 5 percent of an employee's annual earnings put into the plan. Given this estimated calculation, you would never pay more than $40,000 to employees. In fact, you would probably be paying closer to $30,000 because most 401(k) plans average less than 75 percent participation. So not only would you likely save $10,000 annually over a profit-sharing plan, but you would be offering your employees a better way to plan for their retirement.

Let me sound one word of caution regarding 401(k) plans: the savings you realize from a business standpoint may not translate into personal savings for owners. The odds are that you'll be placed in the highly compensated group of the plan, which means you can't maximize the amount of your government-allowed contributions. You can contribute approximately two times as much to your 401(k) account as the average percentage contribution that the rest of your workforce is making. If your average employee contribution is 2.5 percent, then you can contribute 5 percent of your pay. If your annual salary is $150,000, your maximum contribution is $7,500. The government maximum is $14,000, so you're allowed to use only 50 percent of the benefit. Other options may allow you to put more into your personal account. I suggest talking with a reputable agent about the options available to you.

TAILORED PLANS: MATCH YOUR BENEFITS TO YOUR DEMOGRAPHICS

Beyond these standard benefits, a host of other benefits exist, from flextime to sick days to vacation policies to college savings plans. Whatever benefits you choose to offer, each comes with a fixed cost. What's more difficult to determine, though, is the reward based on that cost. In other words, you may spend a given amount on a certain benefit, but your employees view it as irrelevant or trivial. You may spend fewer dollars on another benefit, yet your employees see it as a terrific perk. Don't fall into the trap of selecting benefits based on costs alone: you can maximize your benefit dollars by determining the types of benefits that best suit your employees.

The best way to do this is to determine which of three demographic groups dominates your workforce. To help you do so, here are these three groups, followed by what they typically value most:

Younger workers (18–25, single or married without kids, relatively few financial obligations):
1. Money
2. Money
3. Time off from work
4. Flextime

Middle-aged workers (22–45, married or divorced with families, significant financial obligations):
1. Money
2. Health insurance
3. Time off from work
4. College funds for kids
5. Flextime
6. Retirement

Older workers (45–65, married or divorced with college-aged or grown children, retirement issues):

1. Money
2. Health insurance
3. Retirement benefits
4. Time off from work
5. College funds
6. Flextime

If you have a younger workforce, your benefits probably should skew in the direction of bonuses, short-term profit sharing, generous vacation and sick day policies, and flextime. If your workforce is primarily middle-aged, health insurance is a key concern. If you have an older workforce, health insurance and retirement benefits are critical issues. Most small companies have a mix of all three groups, but it's likely that one group is more dominant than the other two. Your benefits, therefore, should be designed with the dominant group in mind. In this way, you'll get more bang for your benefit buck.

This analysis will also help you avoid spending time and money on plans in which most of your employees aren't particularly interested. For instance, we decided to implement a flextime plan in our company a few years ago. I assumed that this innovative approach would be welcomed by most employees, giving them more scheduling options and also allowing them to work fewer hours for the same salary. We wanted to implement flextime because it would enable us to increase capacity in certain work areas, allowing us to run 24/7. The tradeoffs were that for additional time off, people would have to work 12- and 10-hour shifts when they were here, and more weekend work would be required.

While the flextime plan was generally popular with our younger workers, they only constituted 10 percent of our workforce. About 70 percent of our employees were in the middle-aged range, and they vehemently protested the plan. As a result, we canceled the plan; it didn't make sense to frame as a benefit something that was actually making our employees unhappy.

It's impossible to please everyone all the time. Nonetheless, it's cost-effective to try to please most people at least some of the time. You have a limited number of dollars you can spend on your benefit package, and you want to get the most out of it that you can. Consequently, assess what benefits will really make most of your employees happy and which ones they're just not interested in. Solicit feedback about potential changes to plans, and anticipate objections to changes you're considering. In this way, you will benefit in terms of morale and employee retention while your employees enjoy health, retirement, and other benefits.

4

THERE'S NO ACCOUNTING FOR WASTE

Contrary to what some people might believe, small business owners are generous to a fault when it comes to accounting procedures. The stereotypical image of a small businessperson who knows where every penny of the company's money is going and whose accountant gets involved in shady tax dealings is just that—a stereotype. In reality, many small company CEOs are not sticklers for accounting efficiency.

Some CEOs bend over backward to allow their customers as much time as possible to pay their bills, fearful that a phone call or e-mail reminding them that they're behind might cause the customer to refuse to pay and take their business elsewhere. In other instances, laziness rather than fear causes them to allow slack accounting methods to persist. I know more than one small company owner who has stuck with the same accountant for years, even though that accountant is not particularly good at saving the company money. The owner feels loyalty to this longtime service provider or simply doesn't want to make the effort to find someone new.

If you're serious about saving money and spending it more wisely, however, you'll overcome your fears and laziness and start accounting for every dollar (if not every penny) that flows through your company. What you'll probably find is that numerous opportunities exist to increase the flow of money coming in and decrease the flow of money going out.

GOOD CUSTOMERS, BAD PAYERS: HOW TO HELP THEM PAY ON TIME

Obviously, you want to do everything possible to avoid bad customers, since one typical way in which they're bad is that they pay with agonizing slowness—or they don't pay at all. I'm assuming that most small business owners do thorough credit checks before accepting orders from new customers. It's wise to request that new customers provide names of at least two of their current suppliers so that you can determine how they pay. Sending a standardized form to these suppliers should elicit a response within a day or two. You can also run a Dunn and Bradstreet (D&B) report on new customers (though these reports are not foolproof—we had a longtime customer file for bankruptcy even though their D&B report made them seem stable and reliable). D&B reports are available by telephone or online for a fee.

Ultimately, however, the challenge for most small businesses is not screening bad customers but managing good customers who, for whatever reason, don't pay within a reasonable period of time. Complicating matters, your competitors may have a more forgiving collection policy than you do, making you wary of taking a hard line with customers. The last thing you want to do is turn a bill over for collection when it involves a longtime customer or one with whom you hope to build a long-term relationship.

As an alternative to taking a hard line or doing nothing, consider using the following seven-step slow-pay response.

1. When payment exceeds 45 days, send follow-up copies of invoices on bright pink or red paper. We use this technique—borrowed from another small company we know—with our delinquent customers, and it is tremendously effective. Psychologically, the bright color suggests warning or alarm. It gets people's attention. Similarly, we make sure that the word *invoice* can be seen through the envelope, so that it catches their attention even before it's opened. We've actually had some customers request that we stop sending them invoices on this red paper—my suspicion is that it makes them feel guilty for paying so slowly. Many slow payers aren't bad people who are trying to cheat you. Sometimes, they just aren't particularly prompt in anything they do, including paying bills. In other instances, they are paying slowly for a reason, usually related to financial problems. Sometimes, this "scarlet letter" approach is all that's needed to draw attention to the problem and cause them to pay on time, motivated by guilt or embarrassment or conscience. In still other situations, one person at the customer's company is responsible for slow payment—that person is lazy or disorganized or believes that slow payment is good business. This technique often alerts others in the company to the problem, causing them to speed up payments.

2. Make a meaningful call after the second notice goes out because payment has not been received. Too often, meek, weak, meaningless calls are made to customers with no effect. Typically, you assign a clerical person to make the call, and this individual either doesn't talk to the person responsible for signing a check or is intimidated by the customer. Therefore, make sure that someone with financial responsibility in your company talks to someone with financial responsibility at the company in question. We reserve one week per month in which our controller and accounts receivable clerk call late-paying customers. They are not rude or overly aggressive, but they are firm and make sure customers receive the message that we expect payment immediately.

3. Have the owner phone the most difficult or recalcitrant payers. Some customers don't believe you're serious about collecting the money due until the owner personally makes a call. Psychologically, a CEO's or owner's call tends to carry more weight than one made by the controller. A number of individuals I interviewed also noted that their voice on the phone can frequently prompt a customer to start paying.

I realize that these calls can be tough for some of you to make and that some owners may feel guilty about "bothering" a customer. I understand that guilt—I always feel that way for the first few calls. Then I remind myself that I fulfilled my part of the bargain—I supplied them with good product, at a fair price, and on time. Therefore, a call to determine when they intend to make good on their part of the bargain seems perfectly reasonable.

When you call, make sure to give your name and title right off the bat. Next, ask when you can expect payment. If you don't receive a satisfactory answer, ask to speak to the controller, and if that person isn't available, ask for the owner. Sometimes, nothing happens until two owners speak, despite the best intentions of your employees.

4. Create your own de facto finance charge. When you complain about slow payments, you may receive a letter from a customer along the following lines: "Our corporate office has informed us that they will now be paying all invoices in 60 days rather than 30." You can react by informing them that your corporate policy is to be paid within 30 days; if they refuse to comply, increase your prices by 5 percent. In this way, you cover whatever interest you lose through the slow payment. You'll also find that very few customers will protest this small increase.

5. Offer an incentive for fast payment. Let me qualify this step by emphasizing that I don't recommend offering an incentive for fast payment of money already due. You don't want to set a precedent in which you have to renegotiate the original deal in order to get paid. On the other hand, you might suggest that customers will receive a 2 percent discount on their next order if they pay within ten days.

6. Hold orders or withhold service until payment is made. Because it might be ill received by the customer, it's best to use this tactic sparingly and selectively. If you have a valued, longtime customer who falls behind, you probably owe it to them to exhaust every other possible avenue to collect what is owed before taking this step. In addition, if you're dealing with someone who is arrogant or has a short fuse, this tactic may result in their turning your hard-line policy into an excuse to fire you.

Perhaps the best time to use this approach is when you believe a customer is paying some suppliers promptly and some slowly. In other words, they're taking advantage of certain suppliers because those suppliers allow them to take up to 60 days. When my company stopped entering orders for one customer who was extremely overdue on several invoices, we were holding $10,000 worth of business from being put into work. This made this customer's purchase agent upset, but he also understood our rationale. He knew (though we didn't) that his company was going through a major restructuring and had poor cash flow during this time. As a result, they were stretching out payments to certain suppliers to deal with their cash-flow problems. When we withheld their order, though, the purchase agent urged the owner to pay us quickly, and as a result, they not only paid us but abided by the 30-day rule.

7. Use a collection agency recommended by others. Some collection agencies are incompetent or mediocre. Others are aggressively bad and can cause more problems than they solve. The last thing you want to do is find a collection agency that uses strong-arm tactics to the point that a customer files a complaint against you with the local business bureau or tarnishes your reputation.

Look for an agency that has produced satisfactory results for other business owners you know. Ask them if they have been able to collect on accounts that they had given up on—the ability to squeeze blood from a stone is a valuable one. They should also work on a 17 to 25 percent fee basis.

HOW TO SAVE MONEY BY PAYING BILLS

Many small companies run their accounts payable (A/P) weekly. This is standard practice for a variety of reasons, and because it's standard practice, it's rarely questioned. Consider, though, that you can reap a nice savings just by running your A/P every two weeks. For one thing, the clerk who handles this function will probably gain about four hours per month that can now be devoted to more productive tasks because this shift reduces the clerk's workload. Second, moving to an every-other-week schedule saves on stamps used to mail out checks. In a small company like ours, that means saving about $2,500 annually. In addition, you'll also save some money in bank fees because you'll be writing fewer checks.

Be aware, though, that you may need to modify this shift to every-other-week paying if you're missing certain discounts offered by your suppliers. Your purchasing manager may work hard to get these discounts (I know ours certainly has), and you don't want to undo all of that hard work with this shift. Therefore, give yourself the option of doing a small A/P run weekly to take advantage of accounts that offer discounts.

AUDIT YOUR ACCOUNTING FIRM . . . AND FIND A NEW ONE IF IT COMES UP SHORT

If you talk to a number of small business owners about their accounting firms, you will hear the same story repeated over and over. They will tell you how they used the same accounting firm for years, the accounting firm was perfectly competent and well respected (and may well have been one of the large firms in the area), and then one day they decided to try a new firm. Within the year, they realized savings that they had only dreamed about before. They kicked themselves for waiting so long to find a new firm, adding up in their minds how much money they might have saved if they had made the change five or ten years earlier.

Don't get me wrong. I'm not suggesting you should continuously switch firms or do so just because you want to see how much more another firm might save you. It's just that some small companies settle into comfortable relationships with their accountants and assume that they are asking for trouble by switching firms. They figure that it will be a huge hassle to explain their business to a new firm, to provide them with all of the necessary financials they need, and to form new professional relationships. Thus, even if they suspect that they might be missing out on certain tax-saving strategies or that their firm is overly conservative, they refuse to look elsewhere.

The best way to evaluate your firm is by talking with other small business owners about their firms. Do they have a firm that they feel is creative and aggressive? How much did their new firm save them over the old one? Do they suggest certain strategies or tactics that seem as if they would make sense for your business?

When evaluating your firm, ask: Do they provide the same suggestions and tax strategies year in and year out without any significant changes? Are they overly conservative? Have they regularly helped you take advantage of changes in tax laws or suggested innovative ways to reduce your tax obligation? Do they provide the personalized service that helps them craft strategies geared toward your particular tax situation (or do they have a cookie-cutter approach)?

Over the years, I've found that a sizable percentage of small business owners are extremely wary of both aggressive tax strategies and smaller accounting firms. They believe that if they pursue any strategy that is different or creative, they will immediately become audit targets. Similarly, they place great faith in the largest accounting firms because of their size; they don't see the irony in small companies preferring large accounting firms.

It may well be, however, that a smaller, aggressive firm is better able to save you money. It may take a more flexible approach and be willing to explore options that a bigger firm, set in its accounting ways, refuses to explore. In addition, a smaller tax firm may charge you less than its larger counterpart.

One of the companies I interviewed offered a great suggestion for companies that are reluctant to leave a long-term relationship with an accounting firm because of loyalty and comfort factors. Rather than take the radical step of looking for a new firm, ask a new firm to look at your books for the past two years. Pay them a small consulting fee for their work and hold out the possibility that they may have a larger role in the future. The person who recommended this strategy followed his own advice, and the new firm offered suggestions that eventually saved the company $75,000 in taxes for that year; they also recommended he refile for the previous two years, and this ended up netting the company an additional $15,000.

Recognize that you may not reap such large savings immediately, but the exercise can help you assess whether your current accounting firm is doing a good job. To a certain extent, you need to rely on your business judgment. Don't be tempted by a new firm that promises the moon and stars but can't provide a concrete strategy to reach them. Don't expect that the new firm will identify clear evidence of incompetence on the part of your current firm. Most of the time, the problems have to do not with incompetence but with a current firm's unwillingness or inability to disturb the status quo. They've been doing things one way for a long time; why try something new?

Restructuring the financials is often the recommendation of a new firm, and it makes sense, since some small companies have financial structures that have been in place for generations and are ill-suited to current tax laws. You may also find that the new firm wants to meet with you more often and know more about your business than the old firm. While this may require a bit more of your time and require you to disclose more private information than you're used to, it can benefit you in a number of ways. Meeting with your accountant on at least a quarterly basis can prevent you from making hasty, last-minute decisions right before you file, giving you more flexibility to adjust your tax strategy as events unfold during the year. Providing additional information about your business helps your accountant understand your business at a level so as to tailor strategies to fit with the particular characteristics of your company and industry.

If you decide to look for a new firm, however, be aware of the following potentially costly mistakes that small companies sometimes make during the search and interview process.

Hiring firms because they tell you that their clients have never been audited. This is a sales gimmick and nothing else, suggesting that they are only interested on preying on your fears. Instead, tell them that you assume that over the years some of their clients have been audited. Ask them why they were audited, how the firm helped with the audit, and what the outcome was. This can tell you a lot more about the firm's capabilities than many other pieces of information.

Hiring the first firm you find acceptable. Many small business owners are impatient; they don't want to waste time and energy on a process that is tangential to their core business. As a result, they hire the first firm they talk to or pick a firm after searching through the phone book. It's much more beneficial to network with other business owners and interview anywhere from five to ten firms before making a decision. A hasty, poorly thought-out decision can cost you a lot of money, especially if you hire a disreputable or incompetent accounting firm.

Deciding to use an in-house accounting person to do your business' taxes. I realize how tempting this is, since you figure this individual knows your business better than anyone and can save you the money you'd pay an outside firm. This person may possess great general accounting skills but not be a great tax accountant. More importantly, your in-house person can't examine your books with a dispassionate eye. An employee probably is too close to the business to take a step back and consider all of the tax options available to you. The employee also lacks the mandate to object to practices or inconsistencies that may cause trouble with the IRS.

EXTRATERRITORIAL INCOME TAX EXCLUSION: A GOLDEN, OVERLOOKED OPPORTUNITY

Speaking of accounting firms failing to maximize savings, let me share a story that illustrates the perils of staying with a firm too long. This story also points out an easy and sometimes ignored method for small companies to save on taxes. The extraterritorial income tax exclusion is a U.S. federal tax program available to companies that have international sales, allowing these revenues to be treated at a lower tax rate. Our former accounting firm never asked whether any of our sales were outside of the United States, so we did not take advantage of what turned out to be about $20,000 in annual tax savings. When we discovered this problem, we decided to find a new accounting firm.

When I told my contact at the old accounting firm I was leaving them, I didn't want to burn any bridges, so I tried to be very noncommittal as to the reasons I was leaving. However, he was persistent in asking about our reasons for ending the relationship, so I finally asked him, "Do you know how many of our sales are in Canada?" He didn't know, and I didn't expect him to know, since he was not responsible for the tax portion of their work. I told him, "Well, your tax department doesn't know either. And it could have cost me $20,000 in taxes last year if I had not caught it." (We were able to refile for the previous year.) That pretty much ended the conversation. He apologized and assured me that if we ever changed our minds or needed any other help, they would be there for us.

This benefit will be phased out over the next couple of years, but it may be replaced in another way, and this story just illustrates the importance of knowing whether your accountant is up to speed on this and other current tax issues.

PERSONAL PROPERTY TAX (PPT): THE INS AND OUTS OF CAPITAL EQUIPMENT TAX TACTICS

If you are not a manufacturing company with a lot of capital equipment or a significant amount of inventory, skip this section and go straight to the next one on real estate taxes. However, if you are a manufacturing company that fits into this category, this section is crucial. PPT can really take a chunk out of your profits. Not all states collect PPT, but there may be some other similar form of this tax that will apply to you. In Ohio, PPT is a tax on all of the equipment and the average inventory your company carries. This tax is used to help fund the school systems in the county in which the business is located. The companies hit the hardest by this type of tax are typically manufacturers with lots of capital equipment or companies that must carry expensive inventory, which could also be a manufacturing company.

If this sounds like your company, confirm that you actually have the equipment that appears on your depreciation schedules. Typically, these depreciation schedules are used to calculate at least part of your annual PPT, so the documents need to reflect what equipment is really there. What can easily happen is that a piece of capital equipment becomes fully depreciated, sits on the books for several years, and then is sold or disposed of, but no one notifies the accounting department. Even if the item is fully depreciated, you still pay PPT on this asset for as long as it is on your books.

When we were in the process of purchasing our company, part of the due diligence process of the sale included having us receive a full, updated list of our equipment and doing a full equipment appraisal of everything in the building. When the appraisal came back, I had my controller compare the appraisal list with our accounting records for the PPT calculation to make sure things matched up. I also wanted to make sure that the appraiser had not missed anything of value, since the bank was using our equipment as collateral for our business loans.

We discovered at least 15 pieces of equipment on our books that the appraisers had no record of. I thought, "Well, maybe this guy missed some stuff when he did the walkthrough, or maybe he didn't include it because he thought it had little or no worth."

When we checked the items we thought he had missed, I knew immediately that several of them had not been in the plant for years or at all while I had been with the company. For the rest of the items, we did a quick search through the plant and found only three that the appraiser had missed . . . and they didn't amount to much. The other 12 we still showed on the books were nowhere to be found. Once we cleaned this all up, we were able to eliminate about $1,800 annually in PPT expense.

Similarly, if you have any equipment that is not running, get rid of it so you don't have it on your books. If you are just using it for spare parts, take it off the books and keep the parts.

Here is a cautionary tale in this regard. We've been trying to sell a piece of equipment for the last two years, but we weren't trying too hard. As it has sat idle in the shop, it has lost more value, depreciated fully, and become even harder to sell. At this point, we'll be lucky to receive $5,000 for it. We recently did the calculations and found that we are paying about $1,600 a year in PPT on this machine, so in the past two years, it cost us $3,200 to have that thing sit on the floor! When we checked to see what we would get in scrap material for it, we learned that it would bring about $1,000—so I said, "Go ahead and scrap it before it costs us any more money."

If you have a piece of equipment that is used only once a year, you might find you are better off subcontracting that particular job rather than paying the PPT on that piece of equipment year after year.

In addition, make sure your inventory is valued at the correct amount. Since some calculations for PPT include the average inventory level you carry, be certain you are not carrying any extra or obsolete inventory. This is something you should discuss in detail with your tax accountant to make sure it is being handled correctly.

Finally, here is one additional tactic for you to consider. In many parts of the country, free trade zones, enterprise zones, or buildings exist that offer some type of local tax abatement. If you are not in one of these areas, you might consider moving to one of them, especially if you do not currently own your building.

For example, Company ABC had an annual PPT close to $100,000. It was not able to take advantage of any local abatements or tax shelters to reduce its PPT in its building. However, new and almost-new vacant buildings within five miles of its current location were offering tax abatements for up to 20 years with either a purchase of the building or lease of building space. These abatements would reduce ABC's personal property tax by as much as 80 percent in some cases. That is an $80,000 per year decrease! ABC's owner had to compare this cost savings to the cost of leasing the space, the costs of moving, business interruption, and other factors. The calculations showed that the abatement arrangements would save about $35,000 each year . . . so they went ahead and made the move.

If you think you may be able to realize a similar benefit, start out by calling some commercial real estate agents in your area and explain what you are looking for. They will be able to tell you if such properties exist, how much you could expect to pay per square foot, and the specific terms of the abatements. With this information, you can get a good feel for whether you need to go any further with your investigation. You also should contact your local government officials to let them know that you are considering moving your operation and why. There may be other benefits they can offer to keep your business from leaving. It never hurts to call and ask the question.

REAL ESTATE TAXES ARE NOT SET IN STONE

Small company owners sometimes fail to question whether their real estate taxes are fair. As a result, they miss a terrific opportunity to save money. It's possible that your property is being assessed at a higher value by the county than the appraised market value. For our company in Ohio, real estate tax is about $35,000 annually. In September, the bank had our building and property appraised by a local appraiser, and it came in about $870,000, which I felt was low. Like many small business owners, though, I had more pressing matters to deal with so I didn't do anything about it. Then in February, we received a statement that the abatement for an addition to our building was expiring in 2004 and that our entire building was now being fully assessed for taxes. It also stated that the taxes would be assessed on a property value of $1,370,000! I nearly fell out of my chair. How could there be a $500,000 discrepancy between the assessed value and the September bank appraisal?

I called the county auditor's office and asked what we had to do to appeal the assessment. They told me that we would need to get an appraisal of the property and submit it with the appeal. However, the appeal had to be filed in January. So because I did not recognize this big discrepancy sooner, I had to wait an entire year to appeal. Once completing the appeal process the following year the county did adjust our appraisal value to $935,000 and our taxes decreased $8,000 per year. Unfortunately, some appraisers assign values that seem to be geared to whoever will benefit most from their work. While reputable appraisers exist, don't take for granted that your appraiser is one of them.

Nonetheless, follow these recommendations when considering how your property is appraised:

- If you see an appraisal that does not look right, check it right away, or you may lose the opportunity for any kind of recourse. In this case, we had to wait another year before we could do anything. It might also determine whether a bank will finance a deal on which you are working. Make sure they haven't missed anything if an appraisal comes up short; go through the appraisal with them over the phone so you understand the positives and negatives.

- Keep up with what properties are selling for around you. This way, you can have some idea of whether your assessments are reasonable.

- If you want to contest the value of your property assessment by the county, contact a local bank and tell them you want to establish a line of credit using your current building as collateral. The bank will order an appraisal and will likely end up having you pay for it, which is normal. The bank will use an appraiser it trusts to give a conservative value so that if it ever needs to foreclose on the property, it will easily recover the loan value.

- Once the appraisal is completed, you will be given a copy. Compare this with the county's assessed value of the real estate and see what the difference is between the two. Hopefully, the two are reasonably close. If not, start the process of contesting the assessed value using your recent appraisal.

- Finally, use your instincts and common sense when deciding if you want to challenge an appraisal. Your time is valuable, and you don't want to be spending hours and hours pursuing a new appraisal when in your heart of hearts, you know the most recent one is fair. If, however, you have a good sense of what things are worth and something tells you a mistake has been made, challenge the appraisal.

Bob Kaynes is the owner of the Bronze Baby Shoe Company, a family business in which he represents the third generation. When he received a new real estate tax assessment and it was quite high, he sensed something was wrong. While some areas near him had seen a dramatic rise in property values, the area where his facility is located wasn't one of them. Bob discovered what a number of buildings in his area had sold for recently, and their relatively low prices confirmed his belief that the county auditors had overvalued his building. He appealed the assessment himself, and it was reduced to a figure that Bob found fair.

RESEARCH AND DEVELOPMENT TAX CREDITS: WHY EVEN SMALL, LOW-TECH BUSINESSES CAN QUALIFY

You may not be a huge high-tech company with technicians running around in lab coats and beakers in their hands, but you still may be able to qualify for an investment tax credit. This tax credit has existed since 1983, but until 2004, the U.S. government did not provide clear guidelines on what was allowable. The program is now more user-friendly and requires less administrative work, making it easier to qualify for and understand. This tax benefit is available to most business entities such as C corporations, S corporations, and LLCs. You may qualify if you are engaged in any of the following activities:

1. Investigating new or improved processes in your operation
2. Investigating implementing lean-manufacturing techniques into your operation
3. Investigating changing your plant layouts to improve product flow
4. Experimenting with new processes to improve your product (even the experiments that don't succeed can be included)
5. Developing custom software

The costs associated with any of these areas might include actual wages for everyone involved in the project, some nonwage costs, and contractor costs associated with qualifying activities. You can go back up to three years to claim these credits.

How much R&D expense do the accountants have to find to make it worthwhile to refile your tax returns or fill out all the paperwork for current returns? My tax expert suggested that a company with a minimum of 40 employees was a good starting point, but you should consult an expert or at least someone with a great deal of experience in this field. A standard tax accountant is more of a generalist and knows about all the standard tax laws. However, R&D cost analysis is something of a niche, so it can pay off to make sure you're consulting with someone who has specialized knowledge.

Doug Shull, the head of Transmet Corporation, does a great deal of R&D on his customers' behalf. He noted that many small companies assume that their R&D is simply a cost of doing business when, in fact, they may be able to write off these expenses through investment tax credits if they meet the following criteria:

- Have an engineering department or employees who are responsible for developing new products or designing new processes
- Hire outside consultants to help develop new processes or products

- Conduct studies to determine whether the company should purchase capital equipment
- Incur installation and training costs associated with the purchase of new equipment

Doug notes that some accounting firms that specialize in this area will assess these criteria without charge, and if they find that you should appeal your tax bill, they are paid a percentage of the money that you save.

YOU'RE NOT PULLING A FAST ONE BY EXPENSING YOUR CELL PHONE

I've found that some small business owners are either so concerned about propriety or so scared of getting in trouble with the IRS that they fail to claim all the business expenses due them. Some owners, too, simply don't know what constitutes a legitimate business expense. In fact, if you have a large or conservative accounting firm, they probably haven't told you what you should or could expense to the business as an owner without raising issues with the IRS.

Many gray areas still exist in the tax-accounting world, and if you're a savvy business owner, you'll at least explore the possibilities. You're not doing anything illegal. No one is going to throw you in jail for claiming a car as a business expense that your spouse once used in an emergency for personal transportation. An accountant I interviewed said, "If you don't get audited by the IRS at least once or twice in your lifetime, you're not pushing the limits of the tax law hard enough." This accountant also told me that even when companies are audited, the settlement process is simply a negotiation to settle the situation. In his more than 40 years dealing with clients who were audited, the IRS always settled for something less its original claim.

What business expenses should small business owners consider that they often overlook? You need to talk to your tax accountant to determine which are appropriate for you. Still, I'd like to end this chapter with a list of a few business expenses that are perfectly legitimate but are frequently ignored by small business owners:

- **Cell phones.** Even if you do not use them exclusively for your business, you can certainly expense them to the business. If you own the business by yourself, you may even be able to include your spouse's phone as a business expense if your spouse works for you or provides consultation on business matters. It's a subject worth discussing with your financial advisor.

- **Internet service for your home.** If you have the ability to log on to your business computer system or check your work e-mail account from your home, this service can be expensed to your business. If you're using high-speed Internet service and it happens to be part of your TV cable bill, ask your tax accountant how much of this you can expense.

- **Company car.** This is one most people capitalize on, but they don't capitalize on it sufficiently. Consider the gas used to operate the car and any regular maintenance on the vehicle. You can either figure how many miles you drive for work each year or just have the company pay for your gas and maintenance. Don't ignore your auto insurance. Sometimes, if you pay for it individually (and get reimbursed by the company), the rates are considerably lower than if you bought it through the business. Regardless, there are several options here. Try whichever one gives you the biggest benefit.

- **Farm or garden equipment.** If you own a business that has a yard that needs to be mowed or a driveway that needs to be plowed, all the tools required to do these tasks can be deducted as part of a business expense, even if you also use them for personal purposes.

When trying to decide if something can be expensed to your business, just ask the question, "Do we or could we be using this product or service in the business?" If the answer to this question is yes, then you should strongly consider expensing it to your business or, if you still have questions, raising the possibility with your tax accountant.

5

MONEY
IN THE BANK

Banks often cost rather than save small companies money. Because small business owners don't always give much thought to their choice of banks or the types of relationships they establish, they lose money both directly and indirectly. In terms of the former, they end up paying hidden banking fees. In terms of the latter, they don't take advantage of the networking and other capabilities that good bankers are in a position to offer. Even worse, they may become a victim of a bank that suddenly calls their loans or refuses to provide them with a loan they need to grow or survive.

I've heard some cynical small business executives say that all banks are alike, that they either are so indifferent to their customers or are so hamstrung by a web of regulations that they can't provide the tailored services small businesses want. While it's true that some bankers are indifferent and they operate under many regulations, it's also true that some banks are much better than others. If you do your homework, assess your bank's performance, and take certain precautions, you can put yourself in a position to establish a much more financially rewarding relationship. Let's look at how you can do so, starting with a simple but critical precaution.

TWO BANKS ARE BETTER THAN ONE

In recent years, big banks have hungrily acquired smaller ones, and many banks of the same size have merged. The result of all this activity is that your friendly local bank may suddenly have new personnel and new policies. In some instances, this may have no effect on your business. In other instances, however, it can cause real problems. First, when a big bank buys a smaller one, the new owner may decide that small business loans are not a core part of its business and force you to pay off all debts relatively quickly. Second, the new management may determine that they want to raise interest rates on your debt or change other terms of your loan. Third, the new bank management may renege on your old loan officer's verbal promise to loan you the money that's necessary to open a new office in another location.

It's even possible that you could experience these problems, not as a result of a merger or acquisition but simply because of a change in internal management and the trusted person you used to deal with is no longer there.

Therefore, you should make it your policy to have strong relationships with two banks at all times. This means more than having a primary bank and a secondary one where you do little more than keep some cash. You must establish relationships with key people in each bank—that's *people* plural, not singular. At the very least, have two relationships with managerial-level staff at each bank. In this way, you provide yourself with a cushion in case one person leaves or one bank is acquired.

To impress upon you the importance of these tactics, let me tell you two stories—one horror story and one with a happy ending.

Jim, the owner of a $15 million manufacturing business, had enjoyed a good relationship with his local bank for a number of years. In 2005, though, it was sold to a larger bank, and it could not have happened at a worse time for Jim. Prior to the sale, Jim had decided to bring in venture capital investors to help reduce his debt service with the bank and inject some cash into the operation. He had discussed this strategy with his contact at the bank, and the loan officer approved of what Jim was doing. After the bank was sold, however, a new loan officer took over from the acquiring bank. This individual deemed Jim's strategy "overly risky" and called the loans due. Even though Jim found two parties who were interested in buying the business and offered to help broker this deal for the bank, the new loan officer wanted nothing to do with it. The bank forced him to liquidate all his assets, and he ended up selling his equipment and inventory for pennies on the dollar. If the bank had simply given Jim a few months to sell his company, they probably would have recouped all their money, the business would have survived, and the employees would not have been out of work. The lesson, therefore, is not to get caught with only one banking relationship, since a backup plan can make a huge difference to your company. You may not face the dire consequences of someone like Jim, but you may miss money-making or cost-saving opportunities.

Devin Needles owns a ministorage business and is also involved in real estate investing. Concerned about interest rate volatility on his loans, he attempted to talk with his major banker about the problem. Unfortunately, his banker was unwilling or unable to suggest alternatives to manage this volatility. Fortunately, Devin had established a relationship with another bank, and even though he had given them only a relatively small portion of his business, he had forged a good relationship with a bank executive. As a result of this relationship, this second bank offered Devin a way to save thousands of dollars monthly and shield him from any near-term future interest rate hike. Devin moved most of his business to the second bank, and the relationship has been mutually beneficial ever since.

TREAT YOUR BANKER AS A TRUSTED BUSINESS ADVISOR (AND NOT AS AN ATM)

The overwhelming majority of successful small business owners I interviewed talked about the importance of banking relationships. They didn't simply talk about it in general terms—having a good banking partner to secure a loan, for instance—but in terms of the strong personal relationships with their banking representatives. In a very real sense, their bankers became their consultants, able to advise them about everything from business strategy to investments, from networking to customers. As the cliché goes, banks are often pillars of the community. Because of their stature, they know everyone and have earned great trust and respect from a wide range of individuals. Many bankers are also extremely astute about business issues, especially in terms of what constitutes a wise or unwise move from a financial perspective. Therefore, a good banking relationship often yields the following benefits:

- Access to various human resources in the community, including prospective customers, various advisors (lawyers, accountants, consultants), and so on
- Informed advice about local markets and companies
- Money-saving or moneymaking suggestions about loans, investments, accounts, etc.
- Brokering the sale of a business

Our banker has helped us in many ways, and sometimes this help has been unexpected. For instance, at one point we decided that we needed to buy equipment from Europe. Our banker offered us ways to pay for this equipment by hedging U.S. dollars against the euro, saving us a great deal of money because we were protected against fluctuations occurring in exchange rates at the time. Wayne Brumfeld, the former owner of Muncy Equipment, found a buyer for his business through his banker. After a year of Wayne getting nowhere trying to sell the business on his own, his banker helped him find just the right buyer.

These benefits, however, don't accrue for everyone. To establish a good relationship with a banker requires an investment of time and effort (and, of course, some money) on your part. Specifically, I would suggest the following.

Take your banker out to lunch at least once every other month. You're not going to establish much of a relationship if you just stop by your banker's office and focus exclusively on your accounts or your loans. You need to get to know your banker and let your banker get to know you. In this way, you cease to be just another account number and become an individual in your banker's eyes. A banker is much more likely to go out of the way to help you with tasks beyond setting up a new account if the banker likes and understands you.

Be open and honest about your business. A number of small business owners I know refuse to disclose much information about their business to their bankers beyond the raw numbers. They believe that telling their banker too much can turn the banker against them. One CEO told me he never tells his banker any bad news about his business, for fear that he'll never loan them a dime again. If your banker would respond this way to the first piece of bad news you share, then that person shouldn't be your banker. The more your banker knows about what makes your business tick, the better advice you'll be given. Let your banker understand your fears as well as your hopes and dreams for the business; provide a sense of its history and how it's evolved. Explain what you're using a loan for and how you believe it will increase revenues and make the business more profitable. With this knowledge, your banker can then offer relevant, useful analysis and suggestions. As one business owner told me, when he leveled with his banker about a need for a sizable loan, the banker walked him through the financials and then suggested that he should request an even larger loan to better help him meet his goals.

Don't dismiss your banker just because the banker tells you something you don't want to hear. Some small business owners view bankers with a skeptical eye. They believe they're too conservative or too self-interested to be good business advisors. If you like and trust your banker, however, give the benefit of the doubt. A good, professional banker will tell you what makes financial sense, not what you want to hear. Part of a banker's job is to tell you when a venture is too risky for the bank to invest money in it. This banker should also back up this belief with numbers, demonstrating the logic of the bank's conclusion. Maybe the banker can demonstrate that this additional debt constrains your cash flow too much during the down cycles of your business. Keep in mind that the banking industry is competitive, just like any other type of business, and banks don't like to turn business away. If the bank does turn down your request for a loan, the odds are that it's based on a real concern rather than an overly conservative investment philosophy. Your banker might even be able to suggest alternatives to secure the financing you require, perhaps putting you in touch with a venture capital firm that does business at their bank or suggesting a partnership with another bank client so you can share the risk. Your banker will not suggest these alternatives, though, unless you keep an open mind about your relationship and the banker's motivations.

FEES AND MORE FEES: FIND A BANK THAT IS FAIR AND FLEXIBLE

Banks may charge fees for any number of services such as making deposits, writing checks, accepting customer wires, sending wires, and providing access to online banking services. You may think that these fees are so minor that they are inconsequential. In fact, over the course of a year, they can be significant. If your bank is charging you an excessive amount—if the fees are more than other banks in your area charge—you should either negotiate a lower rate or switch to another bank.

Most small companies, however, are oblivious to these fees. Some banks recognize that many of their customers are oblivious and charge accordingly. For instance, for a long time I had no idea how much we were spending on banking fees until my controller was out sick. When I began doing the financial closes, I discovered that we were spending $850 monthly on these fees. Like most small business owners, I never saw this figure because it wasn't part of the accounts payable statement I looked at; the bank simply took the money for these fees out of our account.

This seemed excessive, so I called my banker and made a rational argument that we were good customers, and that as such, it didn't make sense that we would be paying so much to do business with his bank. He looked at our fees and agreed, knocking $220 a month off our bill for an annual savings of $2,640.

Remember, too, that you have a certain amount of clout in negotiating these fees if:

- You're one of the bank's larger customers.
- You have one or more significant loans with the bank on which you're paying interest.
- You have been a customer of the bank for a number of years.

- You are an influential member of your community and have referred other customers to the bank.

Bring up these points during your fee negotiations, and it's likely your banks will recognize the validity of your position.

LOCKBOXES: A WORTHWHILE INVESTMENT OR AN UNNECESSARY EXPENSE?

Banks charge customers what may seem like a small fee for having a lockbox for their accounts receivable (AR). This is something that we have considered at Peerless Saw Company on at least two different occasions, but we ultimately could not justify the cost of this service. To justify this expense, you need to measure the possible benefit of your AR getting into your account one day earlier, on average. Banks claim you'll gain one day, but I'm not certain if this is always the case. If you figure a lockbox can save you one day, though, you need to figure average daily receivables and know your present interest rate of your line of credit, if you have one. Given these numbers, you can then calculate the annual benefit of having your AR hit your account one day earlier.

The other benefit of a lockbox can be the reduction in time your present AR clerk spends putting the daily deposit together and the time expended on taking it to the bank each day. Unless you are eliminating a position or reducing overtime in some way, though, this isn't really a benefit. If the body is still there, so is the cost. Many small companies like ours don't have one person whose sole responsibility is AR; they usually are handling other tasks such as HR issues and customer invoicing. When we did our calculations, we found that the cost benefit of a lockbox was not justified until our sales were at least $20 million a year. When looking at your numbers, you may come to the same conclusion.

SMALL VERSUS BIG

Some small business owners argue in favor of going with small banks because those banks understand their needs better. Others argue in favor of large banks because they offer more services and have better accesses to business resources. In general, I've found that the largest banks tend to be slaves to rules regarding their risk exposure. They are under intense federal scrutiny, and they find it difficult to make exceptions in your case even when you have a valid argument for making an exception. At the same time, small banks are vulnerable to being swallowed by large ones, so you may think you've chosen a small bank but, in fact, an acquisition quickly turns it into a large one.

In some ways, the small versus large argument is specious, at least from a financial perspective. What you're really looking for is flexibility. In other words, you want a bank that understands what it's like to be a small business owner and how, for example, your best customer's bankruptcy may make it difficult for them to pay you for a few months and make it difficult for you to keep up with your loan payments to the bank during that time. Ideally, you have a banker who is willing to bend the bank's rules about calling loans or issuing stiff penalties when payment isn't made.

Small, local banks tend to be more flexible in this way than larger, corporate-owned affiliates, but it's possible that you've found an enlightened larger bank that possesses flexibility. Before choosing a bank, ask about how flexible it will be if you run into problems or face a crisis. Will it be willing to ignore its standard policies and procedures to help you out of a difficult situation? Does it have a history of using common sense, rather than inflexible rules, in dealing with customers? Talk to some other small businesses that bank with a given financial institution and see what they say.

TAKE THESE QUESTIONS TO THE BANK

Even in smaller communities, you probably have at least a few banks to choose from. In larger ones, you may have a bewildering number of options. I know some small business owners who choose a bank purely by proximity—it's the closest one geographically to their place of business. This might result in a good banking relationship, but this relationship is too important to decide by geography alone.

Therefore, to help you consider all the factors we've discussed before making your choice, ask the following questions:

- Does a prospective banker seem interested in your business? Does the banker ask questions that demonstrate an interest in more than how much money you plan to place with the bank or how much you want to borrow?
- Are the bank's fees reasonable, especially relative to those of other banks in the area?
- Is the bank a victim of a recent takeover or merger; is it changing all its rules and policies to conform to those of a corporation located hundreds or thousands of miles away?
- Is the prospective banker willing to form a real relationship, one that involves regular meetings, occasional lunches, and an honest and open exchange of information?
- Is there a lot of turnover at the bank? Do you have a new customer rep every few months? Are the tellers constantly changing, or do people stay for a long time? How long has the rep who will be handling your account been with the bank?
- Do you know other small businesses that are satisfied customers of a particular bank? Why are they satisfied?
- Is a particular banker well connected? Does the banker seem to know everyone worth knowing and be willing to

give you names of people to contact who might help you achieve business goals?

- Does your representative manifest any or all of the stereotypical negative qualities of a banker: coldness, inflexibility, stickler for following the rules, or disinterest in anything about your business outside of financial matters?
- Is the bank willing to loan you money on fair and reasonable terms? Is it willing to be flexible on these terms if you happen to run into temporary difficulties in the future?
- Does a banker strike you as trustworthy, savvy, and a problem solver?

This last question is obviously difficult to answer based on a single interview. Nonetheless, it's one you should keep in mind as you start getting to know your banker. A good banker can fill many roles in your business life that can save your company money directly and indirectly. A banker who is savvy may be a good sounding board for a promising business venture. A banker who is trustworthy will make good on a promise to give you a loan when you decide to pursue that venture. And a problem solver may come up with ideas for dealing with complex financing problems as your venture takes off.

Use all these questions regularly in your banking relationships, asking them as you try to decide on a banker, as well as during the banking relationship, to assess whether the relationship is saving you or costing you money.

6

UTILIZE SAVVY IN CONTROLLING UTILITY AND INTERNET COSTS

Have you looked at your electric bill recently? Your phone bill? Do you know how much employee Internet usage costs you? Most small business owners I've talked with have a vague idea of these expenses but are in the dark when it comes to specifics. Many times, they are surprised to learn the annual sum of these costs. They are even more surprised to discover that some simple actions can help reduce these expenditures significantly.

If you're going to benefit from the advice in this chapter, though, you must get past the "it's only a drop in the bucket" mind-set. More so than many of the other topics covered in this book, utilities costs often provoke nothing more than a yawn. People feel that turning off the lights and shopping for the best phone deals aren't worth it—that the effort will yield little financial reward.

In truth, this is one of the easiest, most painless ways small companies have to control their costs. When you consider all the things you and your employees can do every day to limit these costs, you realize that you can save thousands of dollars each year with a flick of a switch. Actually, you have to do a bit more, but as you'll learn, this is an area where just a little effort can produce big savings.

SEE THE LIGHT

Do you want to save a few thousand dollars annually just by being vigilant about the use of lighting? Here's all you need to do:

- When you pass by an empty office or work area and you know the person is going to be gone for a while, turn off the lights.
- When you leave for the day, turn off the lights.
- When a conference room or other large work area isn't in use, turn off the lights.
- When you're the last one to leave a meeting room, turn off the lights.
- When all the lights in a work space are blazing and there are only one or two people who require illumination at their desks, turn off all unnecessary lights.
- When people have adequate illumination coming through windows and skylights, turn off the lights.
- When people tell you they prefer small desk lamps to much larger and more extensive overhead lighting, turn off the overhead lights.

If you can communicate this message effectively to your workforce, you will reduce your electric bill dramatically. Unfortunately, most small business owners in the United States are oblivious to energy costs, unlike at least some of our colleagues in Europe. My business partner and I were visiting a manufacturing facility in Germany a few years ago, and when we arrived, they took us to their conference room. As we walked down their corridors to the conference room, I noticed that a number of offices were dark. As I took notice of the dark offices, I assumed that people were on vacation or had been fired.

After we met in the conference room, we were taken on a plant tour. I noticed that the last person out of the conference room turned off the lights. As we walked back down the corridor, I also noticed that one of the "unoccupied" offices was now occupied—an individual was at a desk and the lights were on. We arrived at the plant, where many people were hard at work, and observed their processes. At noon, everyone took off for lunch, and as soon as they had left, all the lights were shut down; the skylights in the shop provided enough light to get around.

As it turned out, this German facility, like others in Europe, is highly energy conscious, and the company looks for every opportunity to reduce energy use. When we returned to this country, I resolved to be more energy conscious. To that end, I noted that one area of our plant operates on only one shift. We figured out how much electricity the lights in that area use during a typical shift. A little math revealed that if we kept the lights off in that area during the two shifts when no one was there, we would save $2,300 annually—which is exactly what happened.

You may have noticed my mention of skylights. Many small business owners have told me that they don't install skylights because they're worried about leaks when it snows or rains or concerned that the expense will be too high. Leaks may have been an issue years ago, but it should not be a problem today if you have a reputable contractor. In terms of expense, certainly the costs may be a bit higher in the short term, but these costs will quickly even out as you rely on natural rather than electric light and your electric bills decrease. You should also be aware that some contractors may try to dissuade you from installing skylights using these rationales. In fact, they often just prefer installing continuous sheets of roofing material rather than having to make the additional effort skylights require. I think it's also worth noting that I recently visited a new

Wal-Mart and noticed that it had installed skylights. If Wal-Mart, one of the most cost-conscious large companies, installs skylights, there must be a financial benefit.

Energy-efficient lighting, too, is a viable, cost-saving option. You don't have to run out and replace all your lighting immediately; that would be a significant up-front expense. You can, however, replace lighting gradually. Wait until a lighting system in an area goes bad—replace old-style ballasts with new, more energy-efficient models, for instance—or target the lighting you use the most as the best place to start. If you ask your energy supplier, you might find that they have existing programs designed to help offset the expense of switching to more energy-efficient alternatives.

If you plan a major shift toward energy-efficient lighting, some lighting manufacturers offer highly attractive incentives to make this type of shift; some utility companies also offer incentives for installing such lighting. Westinghouse, for instance, has been promoting a new lighting system that is much more efficient than the old metal halide or high-pressure sodium fixtures that are found in many factories. The new system, called Westinghouse High Bay fluorescent fixtures, claims to result in a 50 to 75 percent reduction in energy consumption. When we considered the offer, a Westinghouse representative visited our place of business, evaluated our facility's requirements, and did the return on investment (ROI) calculations. In our facility, they estimated an ROI of about 18 months. These calculations are fairly precise: when a light is on for x hours a day, it will use a certain amount of kilowatts of electricity, and when you replace it with a light that uses fewer kilowatts of electricity in the same length of time, you save money.

HEATING UP SAVINGS, COOLING DOWN COSTS

Here are three simple steps every business can and should take to minimize energy costs:

1. Install a programmable thermostat and make adjustments to minimize the operation of the furnace or air-conditioning during off hours. If your employees rarely, if ever, work on weekends, come in before nine, or stay after five, then this is a simple way to cut costs.
2. Make sure the filters in your heating/cooling system are changed regularly. As easy as this is to do, it is also easy to forget.
3. Install downdraft fans if you have high ceilings. Various types of office machinery produce heat, as do certain types of lighting. This heat rises, becomes trapped near the ceiling, and is never distributed to the places people are working. A downdraft fan, however, can circulate this heat to work areas and save on heating costs.

You also can exercise a certain degree of freedom in regulating the temperature of your work areas. Though you don't want to do anything that makes it uncomfortable for people to be in your facility, dialing down the temperature a few degrees in the winter and up a few degrees in the summer probably will have little or no effect on most of your employees. If anyone is uncomfortable, you can always restore the thermostat to its previous settings. You can also give people the option of having a fan or space heater in their area if they really are too cold or hot (or opening windows on nice days, assuming you're in a building where the windows open).

In interviewing small company CEOs, I found that the vast majority of them had never surveyed their employees and asked if the office was too hot, too cold, or just right. This survey is important, since many times, owners wrongly assume that everyone is fine with the current settings. Typically, office buildings are overheated in the winter and overcooled in the summer. You may have an opportunity to lower your energy costs and make your employees more comfortable at the same time.

MANUFACTURERS: STOP YOUR EQUIPMENT FROM BECOMING A DRAIN ON THE BOTTOM LINE

If you have a lot of machinery in your operation, you're going to be using a significant amount of electricity. Fortunately, you have more options than you're probably aware of to reduce your use of electricity. The first option has to do with changing when you run your equipment. As you may know, most facilities are billed based on their peak load. If this peak period occurs at the same time as the energy company's peak usage, your rates will be high. Typically, the peak time for both companies and energy providers is Monday morning. If you run a lot of heavy equipment that requires a great deal of electricity, consider switching the times you run it to off-peak periods. Here are some other tricks that will help you reduce your electric bills:

- If your operation runs all three shifts, start the equipment on the third shift.
- If you are running on just one or two shifts, start the shift at 5:00 AM instead of a few hours later to avoid peak times. Contact your utility company to confirm when its peak is. Most large utility companies have personnel whose specific responsibility is to help customers with these types of issues.
- If you live in a hot climate and run two shifts, determine if it would be possible to run a first and third shift and eliminate the one in the middle (since this second one would take place during the hottest part of the day).

Another worthwhile action is to invest in new motors for equipment that has run on the same old motors for years. Yes, the old motors may be reliable, but they are often enormously inefficient. At the very least, weigh the replacement cost against the energy savings and then make a decision.

Next, if you're relying on a compressed air system, determine if it's the newer screw type or if it has reciprocating compressors. The screw types are much more energy efficient than the reciprocating types. In addition, the screw types require less maintenance. They also are quieter, which indirectly helps the people who work nearby to be more productive, since the reciprocal compressors can create a racket. In fact, when we were installing the new screw types, I was impatient since I was anxious to see how they would perform. When I went down to the floor where they were to be installed, I asked my maintenance staff why it was taking so long. They said they had already been installed. "Then what are we waiting for? Fire it up!" They told me it was already running. I had to place my hand on it to feel the vibration to verify it was going, since it was so quiet.

As you might expect, this screw type compressor costs more than the reciprocal compressor. For us, it took about three years to make up the additional cost, but combined with its quiet operation and lower maintenance costs, it seems worth the investment.

Speaking of compressors, you can reduce costs by monitoring leaks. During the week, it's tough to hear the hiss of escaping air because of the din on the factory floor. Therefore, assign a maintenance person to turn the compressor on and walk around listening for the telltale hiss on a weekend or at another time when everyone is gone. When they find the leak, they usually can fix it by tightening a fitting or replacing a hose clamp.

CONSIDER ALTERNATIVES AND COMPARISON SHOP

I recognize that it's not practical for most businesses to convert exclusively or even primarily to solar or wind power, but cost-effective options exist for small businesses to test at least partial alternative energy solutions. Gasoline prices fluctuate dramatically, sometimes hovering near the $4 per gallon mark, and we're seeing smaller but significant upward trends in prices for electricity and natural gas. The following two alternatives might be worthwhile for small companies to consider:

1. **Install solar-powered lights in your parking lot.** Because of the need for bright lights in many parking lots, this is a good place to start if you're considering alternative energy possibilities. It can save you a small amount of money relatively quickly, and it can also serve as a test for solar power alternatives elsewhere in your facility.

2. **Switch to hybrid energy cars.** One of the small business owners I interviewed has a fleet of 30 cars for his salespeople, many of which are gas guzzlers—SUVs and other large cars. These are the cars his salespeople prefer, but with high gas prices, the costs have become prohibitive. This CEO estimates that the average car is driven about 10,000 miles annually, resulting in annual mileage of about 300,000 miles. The cars get about 20 miles per gallon (which this business owner admitted is a generous estimate). By replacing these vehicles with hybrids, the business owner believes that he could double the miles per gallon, saving a huge amount of money annually. Currently, he's surveying his salespeople about their receptivity to such a move and considering offering financial incentives to each salesperson who is willing to switch. If the average price of gas is $3 per gallon again in the near future, a switch to a hybrid that gets 35 miles per gallon would result in savings of close to $20,000. In addition, this particular company's salespeople travel relatively few miles annually. Many salespeople for small companies drive 30,000 miles or more annually, making a hybrid switch even more financially viable.

I would also recommend finding a company that can evaluate your use of utility-related resources. If you suspect that you're not using energy in the most efficient way possible, call a consultant to investigate everything from electric to water to phone to gas usage. They may recommend a specific alternative energy solution that is ideal for your company.

You should also ask your utility company for help. In most instances, they will be glad to send a representative to your facility who can investigate why a given bill has increased substantially and recommend changes you can make in your operation to reduce costs. Our utility representative, for instance, told us that more often than most people realize, electric meters aren't working properly, resulting in erroneously high bills. By having a representative check the meter regularly, this problem can be avoided.

You should also shop around for alternative suppliers of energy. Increasingly, alternative suppliers exist in all areas of the country. Doing a little comparison shopping may be worth the effort.

THE INTERNET: A POTENTIALLY COSTLY DRAIN ON PEOPLE ENERGY

I'm including a discussion of Internet-related costs because I have found that many small companies experience hidden costs because of the Internet. These costs are similar to costs involving other utilities: poor equipment, inadequate monitoring of use of equipment, or failure to take advantage of more efficient, new technologies. In other words, leaving the Internet on all the time is similar to leaving the lights on: you can be proactive, monitor the usage, and thereby reduce your spending.

While most companies' direct Internet costs are similar, their indirect ones vary widely. I've alluded to how providing unlimited and unmonitored access to the Internet can result in employees wasting hours daily e-mailing and instant messaging friends or visiting non-work-related Web sites. It's also possible that the Internet is costing your company money because of viruses that infect your system or because software hasn't been upgraded.

Given these factors, your MIS staff (or an outside consultant) should periodically do the following:

- Make employees aware that every computer is linked to a server and that, therefore, every Web site visit is tracked by the system. You may have a policy that allows employees to e-mail friends and spend some break time browsing online. That's fine, but making them aware that there are limits to what they do on company time should help them refrain from excessive personal use of the Internet.
- Ensure that each computer has updated virus protection.
- Assess whether everyone has upgraded software so that systems operate efficiently.
- Set up filters to eliminate spam. Some people receive upward of 100 junk e-mails daily, and it takes considerable time to weed out and delete these items.

As you think about the direct and indirect ways you can save money on utilities and technology, keep in mind that small companies that fail tend to be nickel-and-dimed to death. In other words, they usually don't fail because one huge financial catastrophe but bleed to death from a thousand minor wounds. It's not going to kill you if you allow spam to run rampant or leave the lights on overnight, but if you allow a lot of things like this to go on, you're going to lose more than energy.

7

EMPLOYEES: THE ECONOMICS OF KEEPING THE GOOD ONES AND LOSING THE BAD ONES

The war for talent, especially with big corporations who are all vying for candidates from the top MBA programs and the heavy hitters in their respective fields, has been a hot topic in the last few years. You've probably seen stories about companies offering huge financial packages to lure CEOs and other high-performing executives to their organizations.

What hasn't received as much attention is the increasing value of good employees for small companies—and how these good employees are in increasingly short supply. The financially savvy head of a small business recognizes that one of the best ways to keep costs down and profits up is to retain key employees . . . and lose the bad ones. Of course, this is easier said than done. Even in the small business arena, productive, trustworthy employees have more options than ever. They are less likely to stay with your company as long as you want or expect; their ability to get things done combined with their strong character will make them attractive candidates for openings at other companies. Loyalty to a good employer is less likely to keep them in place, even if you strive to provide a quintessential family-like atmosphere where everyone is treated fairly.

The good news is that many of the small business owners I interviewed have found ways to keep their best people and drive away their worst ones. Let's look at some of their suggestions for achieving both goals and the financial implications of these strategies.

SUPERSTARS: GIVE THEM A MILLION REASONS TO STAY

Most small companies usually possess from one to four superstars—high-performing individuals who are absolutely critical to the business. You need to identify these people and reward them with golden parachutes, a financial windfall that they receive if they stay a specific number of years. This should be an all-or-nothing proposition. If they leave even a year earlier than the designated date, they receive nothing. In this way, your superstar employees have the expectation that they will remain with the company, no matter what happens, for a set amount of time.

In my talks with other small business CEOs, the ones who have put this or a similar type of incentive in place have been overwhelmingly positive about its impact on their companies. As one CEO put it, "After I gave John the golden parachute package, he became much more than an employee; he was like a partner in the business and invested even more time and energy than before." Once a high-performing employee feels like a partner, that individual is much more likely to share ideas and information. Before, the employee probably felt like one of "them" instead of one of "us," as a result not telling the owner about problems that were developing or issues that were being talked about by employees. In this new role, however, the employee is much more willing to be open about both problems and the opportunities.

Here are three guidelines for creating an effective golden parachute agreement:

1. **Make the agreement formal.** In other words, write the agreement, have it signed by both parties, and keep it on file. This is important for legal reasons as well as psychological ones. Legally, you want an agreement in place to avoid any misunderstandings down the road and also to protect you and your employee should you die or sell the business before the payment date. Psychologically, the written agreement will create the sense of partnership previously described.

2. **Make the time frame five years.** If it's fewer than five years, you're probably not going to get your money's worth. If it's longer than five years, you're going to have to provide such a large sum that it may also not be cost-effective. At the end of the five-year period, if the employee has responded well to the incentive, consider repeating the process with another five-year offer.

3. **Make the amount approximately half the employee's annual salary.** Obviously, you have some latitude here, depending on a given employee's salary and perceived value to the business. Still, this formula should result in a good ROI. Over the five-year period that the parachute agreement is in effect, it will likely motivate the employee not only to stay in place but to work with a greater sense of energy, commitment, and creativity. In addition, simply having the employee in place to provide continuity and avoiding the huge replacement, search, and training costs for filling the position during that time will save you at least that much. Against the $75,000 golden parachute, it works out to be a great deal for you and your company.

Finally, let me caution you about having narrow criteria to identify your particular superstar. A number of small business owners admitted that it took them a while to realize that their superstars weren't simply their top sales executives. They noted a tendency to designate the salespeople as superstars because their sales skills drive the business—they are the ones with great customer contacts and relationships, and they make a lot of money for their companies. The small business owners added, however, that as important as these sales executives were, they often weren't the ones who were indispensable to the company. Many times, the real superstar was a financial executive who understood the business better than anyone else or the operations vice president who kept the business running smoothly through good times and bad.

Be open-minded when considering who your real most valuable players are. Think about whom you can't do without. Who knows the business better than anyone else? Who helps you keep the profits up and the losses down? Who contributes ideas that solve problems and capitalize on opportunities? These are broad criteria, but they are essential questions to consider in determining who your superstars are.

VACATION POLICIES: A MORE VALUABLE PERK THAN THEY MIGHT SEEM

A good way to keep your best people is to give them pay raises and bonuses that are significantly above the industry norm. Unfortunately, this option isn't always available. In fact, some of the small business owners I talked to admitted that financial realities prevented them from paying some of their top performers what they deserved. In these instances, you need to offer people something else that is significant and compelling to retain them. Vacation time is often the best thing you have to offer.

As many small business owners have discovered, this is a perk that keeps on giving. Unlike most other perks, it costs you nothing—you're still paying people the same salary no matter how much time off you give them. Ah, but what about lost productivity when they take off for four or five weeks? Here's the solution to that problem: offer additional vacation time to your top people who reach all their annual objectives. These objectives must be clearly stated, so there's no doubt as to whether they have been achieved. Once these employees have met their goals, they earn an additional set of vacation days. It's your decision how much more vacation they receive—whether one, two, or three weeks, or more—but the operating premise of this policy is that by achieving their objectives, they've helped the company make a significant amount of money. Even if their absence causes minor inconveniences and others have to cover for them, you come out a winner.

If you wonder whether additional vacation is enough of a perk to keep your key people from leaving, let me share with you an experience I had when I was working for a larger corporation. At the time, I had two relatively new direct reports who had done a terrific job, but I couldn't give them raises because the corporation had recorded only a decent rather than an outstanding annual profit. I was worried that these direct reports would leave if I were to say to them, "Great job. Here's a 2.5 percent raise."

Therefore, I decided to change company policy, which provided new employees at their level with only two weeks of annual vacation. I promoted them to "staff," which meant they automatically received three weeks of vacation. It essentially meant they received that extra week of vacation five years earlier than company policy allowed.

Both of them were so ecstatic about the decision that you would have thought that I had given each of them a $10,000 raise. In fact, one of them told me that the extra week of vacation was worth more than a $10,000 raise.

Keep in mind that vacation time is precious to younger people who like to travel, as well as to individuals with families. When they realize that they can receive more paid vacation with your company than with a competitor, they may be willing to reject a job offer that pays them more but allows them to take off less time.

One caveat accompanies this particular tactic: be aware that it can create animosity among employees who don't receive the additional vacation time. Some of your employees may feel it's unfair that a certain employee receives an additional week or two of vacation while they don't receive anything. In any organization, some employee will always think it's unfair that another received a big bonus, a large pay increase, or even the coveted corner office; it comes with the territory. Still, I would communicate to your employees that at a certain level, when managers reach significant goals, they are rewarded with additional vacation time. Fair and consistent enforcement of this policy should minimize objections and complaints from other employees.

BE FAMILY-CENTRIC IN DEED AS WELL AS IN WORD

In some small companies, the notion that employees are family is a joke. Though the company literature and the CEO's speeches may try to propagate this myth, everyone knows that the organization will not spend one extra penny on its employees or implement programs or policies that they have requested. The organization is perceived as cold and money-hungry, and people often are eager to leave these companies at the first available opportunity.

To counter this perception and make employees feel that you really do regard them as part of a corporate family, consider the following measures that other small businesses have implemented successfully.

Set up a college fund for employees' sons and daughters. This is enormously easy to do, costs very little, and is something most of your employees with children will appreciate and participate in. For instance, one small business owner I interviewed wanted to offer some kind of incentive to keep his sales manager happy and with the company for at least the next five years. The owner agreed to set up a college fund for each of the manager's young daughters, ages one and four, with the proviso that the manager had to stay with the company for at least five years to use this fund. The owner started what is called a College 529 Plan, which allows money to be deferred pre-state tax for each child. When the child starts college, the money is pulled from the fund, without any taxes on earnings, and used to pay for all college expenses. This owner set up a plan in his own name with the manager's two daughters as the beneficiaries. The owner would then deposit $2,000 into each account annually. If the sales manager stayed with the company for five years, the owner would transfer ownership of the plan over to him. If the manager left the company any earlier, he would receive nothing, and the owner would either change the beneficiaries of the fund or cash it out.

Buy life insurance for employees. Again, this is a relatively inexpensive investment that communicates you care about your employees and their families. You may not realize how inexpensive some types of life insurance are. For example, you can purchase a $500,000 term life insurance policy for less than $1,000 in many instances. You can also give employees the option of retaining this insurance policy even if they leave your company; they simply pay for the policy themselves. Most won't exercise this option if they leave (so it doesn't provide an incentive to leave), but while they are with the company, they appreciate the gesture, as do their families.

Offer sabbaticals. Borrow a page from academia and offer people leaves of absence for specific reasons: personal problems (death, divorce), educational programs (special university courses), travel, and so on. Clearly, you can't offer sabbaticals to everyone at any time; small companies are delicate mechanisms, and you can't take out a cog here and a wheel there and expect to continue to operate smoothly. This should be a perk for longtime employees who have performed well. Some of them may simply need a break after many years of loyal service, while others have problems to solve or opportunities to capitalize on. In any case, the opportunity to take a sabbatical is much appreciated by employees in a variety of circumstances.

Provide work-at-home options. Again, this isn't possible for all employees, especially if they're required to be on the factory floor or if their physical presence is absolutely essential on a daily basis. At the same time, some people will be able to be just as productive working at home part- or full-time as if they were to come into the office. With tools such as e-mail and videoconferencing, this is a viable option in the right circumstances. It can be an especially valuable arrangement for parents who have very young children and want to be able to spend more time at home. We've also found that customers have no problem dealing with at-home employees—they just want to get a question answered or problem solved. For instance, when our receptionist takes the call from a customer or supplier for a work-at-home employee, she forwards the call to this individual's desk phone, which can forward that call automatically to an office at home or a cell phone on the road. Employees working at home are logged into our server at work just as if they were sitting at their desk in the office, enabling them to give the customer or supplier the information needed. The customer often doesn't even know that these individuals are not at the office. In fact, I know a partner with a law firm who decided that she had had enough of the big-city life and was moving to Montana. Her firm worked out a deal where she would work from her house in Montana, and none of their clients even knew she had moved until they asked to meet with her. It took a very short time for her to prove that she could provide the same quality of work from over 1,000 miles away as she could if she were sitting at a desk in the big-city office.

Offer flex time. For a variety of reasons—many involving family issues, some people prefer a more flexible schedule than a nine-to-five, five-day-a-week routine. Once again, you can't offer this benefit to everyone. Some employees, however, don't need to be there when everyone else is there. You may have a great financial person who has just had a baby and is trying to be at home when his wife is at work. She has flextime, and if he had it, they could juggle parenting responsibilities without having to put their child in daycare. This financial person could come in on weekends and work afternoons and early evenings (or whatever schedule makes sense). Many big companies have concerns about flextime and work-at-home situations, certain that people will be less productive if they're not being monitored constantly. As a small business owner, though, you probably know your staff better than a manager at a big company does, and you can make a good guess about who will be responsible working under a flextime system.

LET YOUR EMPLOYEES COMPARE APPLES TO APPLES

The most common reason people leave small companies is that they feel they are underpaid. When the job market is tight, this feeling usually doesn't translate into action. When jobs are plentiful and unemployment figures are low, though, you can easily lose a number of "underpaid" employees. In the late '90s, when the employment rate in our area was 4.2 percent and the Sunday jobs section was filled with ads, we lost some good employees, all of whom felt that they were underpaid and wanted higher salaries.

We wanted to assess whether our people really were underpaid. To that end, we contacted the Employer Resource Association, of which we are a member; they provide detailed wage and benefit information for different industries. After reviewing this data, we found that our wages were comparable to the industry average and that our benefit package was more generous than that of most small companies in our area.

We took advantage of this information by creating a spreadsheet for each employee, showing the dollar value of their individual benefits as well as their wages. We also provided them with the wage and benefit data about other small companies in our industry and area. In this way, they could compare apples to apples—a given employee might receive a salary that was $1,000 less than in a comparable company but also receive $10,000 more in benefits.

Don't keep this information secret. Many small company owners are a bit paranoid about sharing any of this information with their people for fear that they'll see that the company isn't providing a benefit that someone else is offering or isn't paying as well as the industry average. Clearly, if you're paying people low wages and offering few benefits, you don't want them aware of these facts. However, if you pay a fair wage and try to offer a reasonable benefit package, it's in your best interest to give your employees all of the economic facts and give them a context for comparison. In this way, you might keep a good employee who would otherwise have left under the mistaken notion that "the grass is always greener."

COSTLY EMPLOYEES: FIRE THE ONES WHO ARE MORE TROUBLE THAN THEY'RE WORTH

I know how difficult it is to fire people, but I have also learned the hard way that certain employees cost the company far more than is apparent at first glance. Some people are simply unproductive or unsuited to their positions, and firing them is the obvious choice. Some employees, however, may be mediocre or even moderately productive, but they cost you more money than you can imagine. Use the following checklist of costly traits to evaluate your employees.

____ Complains constantly about the company; makes regular, cynical comments about the company's culture, pay scale, or leadership.

____ Takes pride in doing just enough to get by; brags about having the system beat.

____ Uses charm and political savvy to convince supervisors that he or she is doing a good job but is highly manipulative and duplicitous.

____ Enjoys causing trouble; gets in verbal scrapes with other employees; people complain that this person is difficult to work with.

____ Takes advantage of the company in numerous ways; falsifies expense accounts; lies about absences; takes off early whenever it may not be noticed.

____ Likes to manipulate other people; enjoys provoking conflict between fellow team members and antagonizing colleagues.

____ Sabotages projects and programs, either through lack of effort or by deliberately making mistakes or offering misleading information.

If a specific employee earns two or more check marks, this is probably someone who doesn't belong with your company. I understand that it's difficult to fire a longtime or productive employee, no matter how many check marks that person has. Sometimes, too, people aren't as cut-and-dried in their negative behaviors as this checklist portrays. Employees may complain about the company once or twice a week but be model citizens the rest of the time. You can find yourself on the fence about someone despite the check marks. In these instances, you must rely on your instincts: your gut will often tell you what to do when your head is uncertain. It may be that coaching is a better approach than firing for a given employee or that you need to give an employee specific goals to meet.

Above all else, don't drag out a bad situation with an employee who receives lots of check marks. Don't offer innumerable second chances, put the employee on various probations, or threaten termination if a behavior doesn't stop. Dragging out bad situations in this manner does no one any favors, and it may expose you to costly litigation because you didn't act decisively—your bad employee may take advantage of your "kindness" and turn it against you in the form of a wrongful termination lawsuit.

Years ago I read a book that offered the following advice: "Fire fast and hire slow." If you need any support to follow that adage, think about the indirect costs of having cynical, lazy, manipulative, and game-playing employees. They can turn good, productive employees into average ones with their negative talk about the company; they can alienate customers and change the way they view the company; they can alienate suppliers with whom the company has been on good terms; they can create an atmosphere on a team or in any work group that diminishes its commitment to goals as well as its energy and creativity. It's not always easy to be sure how all this translates into dollars, but the loss is significant.

The bottom line is that if you can eliminate a few of your most costly employees and retain a few of the ones who make the most money for the company, then you're bound to end up on the plus side of the ledger.

8

DON'T SELL YOURSELF SHORT: CONTROLLING SALES AND MARKETING COSTS

Many small companies have an almost religious adherence to certain sales and marketing practices, especially if business is good. They always take out three ads annually in a trade publication, or they routinely provide salespeople with a company car. No one questions whether these sales and marketing expenditures are cost-effective because they have become set in stone; no one even considers whether a more cost-effective alternative exists.

Some small business owners have taken radical steps to reduce their sales and marketing costs. Some have stopped advertising completely. Others have reduced their sales staff by 50 percent or more by relying on e-commerce and other virtual tools to sell their products. Still others have outsourced their entire sales function.

I'm not suggesting you need to consider these radical approaches to saving money in this area. In fact, I'm going to start out with some incremental tactics to reduce costs and then, in the second half of the chapter, examine the possibility of making more dramatic cuts.

GIVE YOUR SALESPEOPLE WHAT THEY NEED, NOT WHAT THEY'VE ALWAYS HAD

There's an adage that you have to spend money to make money, and there's no question that your salespeople must incur certain expenses to be successful. Specifically, they probably need to spend money on travel, lodging, and cell phones if they're going to land and keep customers. At the same time, they may be able to land and keep the same number of customers if you make judicious changes in four areas. Let's look at each one and some easy changes you might make.

Vehicles

Many small companies have taken a cue from larger corporations and have leased cars for their salespeople. Years ago, this was standard practice. Now, some companies have recognized that this can be an unexpectedly costly arrangement, especially when salespeople do more driving than anticipated. For instance, we used to lease cars for our employees. These leases always had huge penalties for exceeding mileage limits. When I started with Peerless Saw Company, we had three salespeople with car leases set for 20,000 miles annually, but our employees put between 40,000 and 50,000 miles on them. We incurred about a $7,500 mileage penalty per car.

We now have our salespeople buy and maintain their own cars. We pay a flat amount monthly as a car allowance and reimburse each salesperson for auto insurance premiums. This has reduced our overall insurance by about $1,500 per year as well as reducing some of our liability exposure. Consider adopting a similar policy on salespeople's cars if you're still leasing, particularly if your employees are incurring mileage penalties.

Second, if you have five or more salespeople, stop paying for their gas and instead get them fleet gas cards. BP, Amoco, and other companies make these cards available, offering customers discounts if they supply their salespeople with their credit cards to pay for gas. The discount varies based on the volume of gas you use, but typically, the range is from 3 to 5 percent. In addition, some credit card companies offer a 2 percent discount on gas purchases if you use only a certain brand. It may not seem like much, but the discount can add up to significant savings over the course of your salespeople's travels.

Travel Expenses

Most salespeople don't spend excessively on purpose. They simply don't think that much about what they're spending because it's not their money. There are steps you can take, though, to get them to be more conscious of what they're spending and consider less expensive options. Your salespeople need to know that they can impress a customer without spending $200 on lunch. In fact, some customers prefer modest expense account lunches, figuring that one way or another, this cost will be passed on to them.

How do you encourage salespeople to think about what they're spending and opt for less expensive alternatives when appropriate? Here are two suggestions:

1. Have them use a company credit card to pay for everything. When people know that everything they spend will be itemized and reviewed by a supervisor, they will think twice before taking their smallest customer to the most expensive restaurant in town. They won't become cheapskates (nor do you want them to be), but they will at least reflect on whether an expense is a good investment in making a sale or keeping a customer happy or if it's an unnecessary extravagance.

2. Give salespeople a direct, understandable incentive to cut sales-related costs. If you try to convince salespeople that the future of the company depends on their keeping spending

down, you probably won't get much of a response. If, on the other hand, you offer to share with them whatever savings they help produce, they will probably be much more responsive. Last year, we reduced our sales-related costs by $2,200 per salesperson by sharing 50 percent of the savings with them. In other words, if a salesperson reduces sales-related spending by $10,000, then that salesperson receives $5,000.

Cell Phones

Perhaps there are salespeople out there somewhere who don't value their cell phone above all other possessions, but I haven't met them. Cell phones have become the lifeblood of every type of salesperson, and as such, each one has particular preferences designed to facilitate a particular selling style and customer requirements. I would urge you not to buy the cheapest cell phone and service for your salespeople, since it is unlikely to meet their needs. At the same time, I would recommend that you figure out what those needs are. Specifically, ask your salespeople to answer the following three questions:

1. What are the average number of minutes you use per month? Do you ever exceed these minutes? How many months in a given year do you exceed them? How many more allowable minutes per month would prevent you from exceeding your limit?
2. Does the service you currently have cause you to lose calls frequently, infrequently, or never? Do you find yourself unable to get a signal in certain areas when you're on the road?
3. What features on your phone are most useful and are indispensable to doing your job well? What features do you rarely, if ever, use?

To help you answer the previous three questions, consider what happened when my partner bought his first cell phone for business use. He set up his account for 500 minutes per month, but when he exceeded his limit by just a few minutes, the rates increased dramatically. Monitoring his bills, we determined his average monthly use was around 650 minutes. Upping his minutes to 1,000 monthly was actually cheaper than staying with the 500-minute plan and paying for the extra minutes.

By answering these questions, your salespeople will supply the information you need to find a more cost-effective phone and provider. It's possible that everyone is happy with what you're currently providing, but it's more likely that you can save at least $1,000 monthly by making changes—changes that also will make your employees happier with the cell phones and service they're using. One of the small business owners I interviewed, for instance, told me that he had always assumed that his salespeople required a trendy, feature-loaded cell phone; he figured that they wanted to impress their customers with this brand of cell phone and that it provided them with all sorts of communication options via the Internet. Because of the questionnaire, however, this business owner discovered that most of his salespeople believed the trendy phone was a waste of money and that they would much prefer a less expensive phone with a few key functions as well as a higher number of maximum minutes.

Speaking of minutes, it's wise to shop around to find a provider that offers the best rates. We have a salesperson in the southern United States who receives 3,000 minutes for $150 monthly, while our West Coast salesperson gets the same number of minutes for $129 per month from a different carrier. Again, don't automatically take the cheapest rate, since the cheaper company's coverage may be inferior or its contract may contain provisions that make it less desirable, such as a rate increase after an introductory period. Still, the odds are that if you shop around for the best service deals, you can save some money.

Finally, require that your salespeople use a hands-free device. The cost is relatively low, and the long-term benefit is high. Your salespeople probably do a lot of customer and prospect calling while driving, and a hands-free device is a good investment given that frequent usage.

Hotel Expenses

Here are two quick pieces of advice that will save you money with very little effort on your part:

1. **Look for regional chain hotel deals.** This is ideally suited to companies whose salespeople cover specific regions of the country. Many of the small company executives interviewed agree that these smaller, regional chains usually offer better deals than their national chain counterparts. Your salespeople may prefer to stay at one of the huge chains because of the name or because it offers a superior bar or restaurant, but if the regional deal can save you even $500 per salesperson annually, it's a better option.
2. **Find hotels that offer free breakfasts.** In recent years, the number of hotels that have moved from free donuts and coffee to full continental breakfasts has risen dramatically. The odds are that your salespeople can find a nice one where they stay. If they do, you will no longer be receiving expense account forms from a salesperson indicating $300 a month spent on breakfasts.

This last point reminds me of an experience I had with a free hotel breakfast, an experience that communicates you can find a wide variety of lodging deals if you're willing to explore options. I stayed at a Comfort Inn in West Virginia recently for $69 per night, and their breakfast included toast, pancakes, cold cereal, grits, apples, melons, and the best homemade biscuits and gravy

I'd ever had. Even better, those biscuits had been homemade a few hours earlier.

For a salesperson who has been working hard and been on the road a while, this is a great perk. Using the Internet and talking to other salespeople who have traveled extensively in a given area, you can discover many different types of deals that will save your company money and be greatly appreciated by your employees.

ARE YOUR SALESPEOPLE EARNING THEIR KEEP?

Now let's move on to some areas where much bigger savings are possible but where bigger and often riskier decisions are required. First, let's examine the possibility of changing your traditional, and probably extremely expensive, sales structure. Many small businesses pay their salespeople handsomely, and they may well deserve every penny they receive. These salespeople not only maintain and grow a healthy customer base, but they generate positive gross margins.

What I've discovered in my own business and in many of the companies whose presidents I interviewed, though, is that it is easy to fall into the overestimating trap. In other words, companies are so dependant on their salespeople that they overestimate those employees' value to their companies. I'm not going to tell you something you know far better than I do—how to evaluate the performance of your salespeople—but I can tell you that you may be able to make changes that can save you five or six figures annually.

The key is determining the following:

1. Is a salesperson doing a good job maintaining your customer base?
2. Is a salesperson doing a good job growing your customer base?
3. Is a salesperson providing you with a positive gross margin?

Don't automatically assume that the answers to these three questions are yes. In some small companies, customers feel loyalty to the entire organization, to everyone from the CEO on down. Maintenance of this customer base is a result of great service, great products, and fair prices. They have been good customers for years, and it doesn't require an outside salesperson making maintenance visits to keep them as good customers. If you have a salesperson who isn't generating much new business and is spending a lot of money to keep existing customers satisfied, you may want to consider eliminating this salesperson and using inside sales reps instead.

Susan is the owner of a Midwestern software firm that has been in business for 18 years and has a solid customer base. Early on, the firm's salespeople were critical in growing the firm and establishing relationships with customers. Over time, however, the accounts pretty much ran themselves. The sales reps still made visits to the customers, who were located across a ten-state area, but Susan gradually realized that she could handle at least half her customers using inside salespeople. She found that three of her salespeople in particular were doing very little in terms of generating new business and were also costing the company a great deal in terms of their expenses and salaries—one of these salespeople had been with the company for 15 years and was making close to $150,000 annually. At one point, this salesperson had helped build the business, but this person had been coasting on that past success for a number of years. Though it was difficult, Susan eliminated these three salespeople and appointed internal employees to take over their responsibilities. This had no negative repercussions on customer relationships, and it saved the company over $300,000 each year.

I want to emphasize that I'm not advising you to fire salespeople left and right to reduce costs. Instead, I'm suggesting you take a hard look at the three factors mentioned earlier and then determine if a salesperson is justifying the salary you're paying. It's also possible that instead of eliminating salespeople, you should explore different ways of reducing your sales costs. For instance, here are some tactics we've found to be effective in this regard:

- Offer salespeople a 50 percent commission on the first order from a new customer. Obviously, you don't make money directly or reduce costs from this tactic. What you will do, however, is motivate your sales force to generate new business. As you probably know, the long-term value of a good customer is worth sacrificing commission on that initial order.

- Keep salespeople on salary to start them out, and as they establish themselves over the first couple of years, gradually move them to a commission base. Most small companies want their salespeople on commission, but if they start salespeople off this way, they end up losing potentially good employees who can't make it on commission alone at first. In this way, you help people learn the ropes and gather the experience and contacts necessary to do well on commission. In the process, you reduce money committed to salaries without hurting the business.

- Use a base salary with a quarterly bonus structure on top of the salary:
  - Meeting quarterly budget goals by product line; if they exceed budget, they can earn additional money so that pay does not top out and demotivate the salesperson.
  - Overall territory development—this essentially means measuring how well they establish sales relationships in a given area.

GRASSROOTS RESEARCH: HOW TO MEASURE YOUR MARKETING EXPENDITURES

It's likely that you can't afford or simply don't want to spend the money that big companies spend on research. As a result, you don't have the data that can drive your marketing expenditures in the most profitable direction. You haven't conducted an in-depth survey of customer buying habits or had a firm analyze your advertising's effectiveness.

Even if you spent the money on a research firm, the expenditure might not yield as productive a result as if you conducted some grassroots research. Specifically, following is some research that's relatively easy to do and will go a long way to making your marketing expenditures that much more effective.

Survey new customers about how and why they're buying from you. This is so simple to do, yet a number of small business owners admitted that they had no idea why customers chose them and how they heard about the company. This is especially true during good times when new customers seem plentiful. No one considers why they have become new customers, since the illusion is created that there will always be "plenty of fish in the sea." It's only when the new customer flow dries up that people become eager for this new customer information. When I started working at Peerless Saw Company in 1995, I found out we were spending nearly $23,000 per year advertising in the Thomas Register, most of which was for our laser-cutting business. This seemed like a huge amount of money, given our company's size. When I started asking our sales team how much business we generated from this advertising, no one had any idea. So I had them start tracking where all our new sales leads (quotes and orders) came from. We tracked this for at least a year, and to my surprise many of our leads and new orders were coming from the Thomas Register. In the end, we kept advertising in the Thomas Register, but we did narrow our focus, reducing our advertising dollars by $7,000 the next year without negatively affecting the business.

Don't wait to unearth these facts about your customers. You have a limited marketing budget, and if you want to maximize it, find out the following when communicating with new customers:

___ Why are you buying from us rather than our competitors?

___ What about our product, service, or company reputation made you buy from us?

___ Where did you initially hear about us (a cold call from a salesperson, a referral from another customer or supplier, a visit to our Web site, an ad, a mailing piece, or an article in a trade publication)?

The odds are that the answers to these questions will surprise you. For example, one company found that the vast majority of their new customers came through referrals from three existing highly satisfied and generous customers. Another small business discovered that their new customers chose them over the competition because they had a word-of-mouth reputation for going beyond the call of duty to solve problems when they surfaced.

Based on this information, you can do everything from playing up your sterling reputation in a trade ad to rewarding the customers who are providing you with great referrals. You can also eliminate or reduce marketing expenditures that don't seem to be paying off.

Survey prospects who choose competitors over you as to why they did so. This means calling them after the fact and asking them why they are buying from your competitors rather than you. What about a competitor's product, service, or reputation was superior to your product, service, or reputation? Again, this will give you valuable data that you can use to reconfigure your marketing expenditures.

Keep this information in the line of sight: This grassroots research is worthless if no one knows about it. Don't gather this information, have a meeting about it, and then file it away in a dusty cabinet. E-mail it to all your salespeople. Post it on your Web site. One of the company presidents I talked to maintained a large chalkboard display in the conference room that listed every new customer and the source of that customer. It was constantly updated and used for everything from executive-level marketing discussions to informal conversations about salespeople's performances.

Gather data from customers about trade shows. I cannot count the number of small company presidents who, when I asked why they went to a given trade show, responded, "Everyone in our business goes," or words to that effect. Similarly, those who exhibited did so on the assumption that it was the right thing to do, since they and their competitors had been exhibiting for years.

We exhibit at and attend trade shows, and they do not result in a lot of new business for our company but typically, we connect with over 100 existing customers at each show we attend. We also find it helpful to see what the competition is doing. At the same time, sending a contingent of employees to a show will probably cost you a few thousand dollars. It makes sense to ask your customers about their attendance at shows. Who specifically (a decision maker?) attends the show? Do they regularly find suppliers or make buying decisions at these shows? Do they pay special attention to the exhibitors?

Wait until the last second before committing to an exhibit. Some trade shows can't fill all their exhibit spaces, and as a result, they sometimes offer last-minute discounts so they don't have empty spaces. Obviously, if a show is clearly important to you, you don't want to wait until the last minute and risk losing a place in the show. In other instances, though, you may save a large amount of money when a show decides to hold a fire sale on exhibit space.

CAPITALIZING ON SELLING ALTERNATIVES

Some small businesses have been slower than larger companies about taking advantage of new selling techniques and technologies. In some instances, this caution is warranted. For certain products and services, nothing beats a personal visit from a salesperson. For other products and services, trade magazine ads are the most effective marketing vehicle.

In other instances, however, small companies overlook nontraditional sales and marketing methods. No doubt you're aware of at least some of these methods. *E-commerce* has become a business buzzword, and most small companies have Web sites that convey and capture information or sell a product. You've seen pop-up ads and perhaps even bought a piece of used equipment online.

What you may have avoided doing, though, is testing some of these alternative selling tools yourself. It's a good idea to explore the possibilities, especially in terms of how they might save your company money. The following are just a few of the alternative selling approaches small business owners have noted during my research:

- **Linking Web sites to expand customer base.** Two companies will agree to feature links to each other's Web sites. Typically, a customer and supplier make this agreement. As a result, they each reach an audience that they might not otherwise reach with their selling message, at no cost to either of them.

- **Using mailing pieces to drive prospects to Web sites.** Some small business owners said that direct mail had never worked for them in the past but has proved to be an effective tool to increase Web site traffic. While prospective customers would not respond to a mailing with a phone call, they were willing to visit the company's site.
- **Online seminars.** These companies sent invitations to prospects and/or customers, requesting their virtual presence at the unveiling of a new technology, product, or service, or offering a free seminar about how to maximize the use of an existing product. They recognized they couldn't expect people to travel to a specific location for a seminar but that people might be tempted to visit an online seminar. In this way, they captured names of prospects for their salespeople and earned a great deal of goodwill when the seminar communicated valuable information.

9

AVOID MANUFACTURING MORE COSTS THAN YOU ALREADY HAVE

If you're purely a service provider, feel free to skip this chapter and go on to the next one. If, on the other hand, manufacturing represents at least part of your business, this chapter is absolutely essential. If you're running a manufacturing operation, you're probably thinking that you're doing everything possible to keep these costs in line. No doubt you've taken some steps to do so. Perhaps you've started buying used rather than new machinery. Whatever you're doing, though, you probably haven't done enough. You have hundreds of options for controlling or reducing manufacturing costs, from techniques that cut down on materials expenses to process refinements.

These options have been tried and tested by small business owners like you. I'm not going to lecture you on Lean Manufacturing, Kaizen, Six Sigma, or any of the other concepts that are popular among academics and *Fortune* 100 manufacturing vice presidents. There's nothing wrong with these concepts, and clearly, their popularity indicates that they can be useful in some contexts. However, the jargon associated with these manufacturing approaches and their lack of relevance to many small business owners make them tangential to our discussion here.

I want to share with you the nuts and bolts of manufacturing cost reduction. My approach is similar to the way I approached the idea of "empowering employees" when I heard about it from a professor as an MBA student. After he used this phrase repeatedly, I asked, "Isn't your definition of empowering employees the same thing as just allowing people to do the things they know how to do to get the job done the best way possible?"

"Well, yes," he said.

You can expect a similarly theory-free, jargon-free approach to reducing manufacturing costs, starting with the basic subject of raw materials.

FRESH THINKING ABOUT RAW MATERIAL SPENDING

Some of the small business owners I talked to were proud of their longstanding partnerships with suppliers. They talked of the trust and open communication that defined these relationships. That's great, but how much are you willing to pay for a wonderful relationship with one supplier? Is it worth losing $5,000 annually? $10,000? More?

In this day and age, there's nothing disloyal in shopping around for raw material suppliers. In fact, in a volatile environment where suppliers can go out of business overnight or raise prices by 50 percent because of their own financial issues, you would be taking a big risk by not investigating other suppliers. It's also a risk to believe that all material prices are fixed and nothing is negotiable. More than ever, suppliers are willing to work with you and consider options to keep your business. Given all this, you should explore the following cost-saving tactics.

Maintain a minimum of three suppliers for your materials. It's fine to have one primary supplier and two secondary suppliers, but the key is having backups in case anything happens to your primary supplier. One of the company presidents I talked to had a major supplier go bankrupt suddenly. One day the supplier was doing fine, the next day it was on the edge of financial ruin. As a result, the company would have been in deep trouble if it hadn't had two secondary suppliers to pick up the slack.

With transportation costs shrinking and trade barriers disappearing, more suppliers from all over the world are available to you. Keep an open mind about new suppliers and make a continuous effort to be informed about who the new suppliers are and what they're offering. In this way, you'll protect yourself in case a relationship with a current supplier goes bad, and your company will also have lower-cost options. In fact, if you tell a current supplier you're happy that you found another supplier offering the same material for less, the odds are that your current supplier will match this lower price.

Push suppliers for early payment discounts. We save about $22,000 annually by requesting these terms. Don't expect your supplier to volunteer that these are available. In fact, you may be the first customer that requests these terms. Be aware, though, that some suppliers are weary of slow-paying accounts, and they are more than willing to offer early payment discounts if someone requests them. Others may be more reluctant, but if they believe you will take your business elsewhere, they may make this concession.

Some small business owners protest that the company's cash flow isn't great and that it can't commit to early payments. If this describes your company's situation, consider opening a line of credit to capitalize on these discounts. For instance, if a bank offers a line of credit at 8 percent, it would still be to your advantage to do it. Suppliers often offer 2 percent net ten-day terms. With these terms, you will save a significant amount of money. In fact, until the line of credit interest reaches 24 percent (an unlikely occurrence in the near term), early pay discounts are still a great deal.

Request a consignment arrangement. If you can get suppliers to agree to consigned stock, you can both improve your cash flow and take advantage of early pay discounts more easily. Admittedly, some suppliers will not want to get into a consignment arrangement, even though it makes perfect sense for them as well as for you. In essence, this deal allows you to keep a supplier's products in your inventory, and you're billed only as the products are used.

We have a supplier with whom we have a consignment agreement. While the tradeoff for this agreement is that their pricing is 2 or 3 percent higher than that of other suppliers, we more than make up for that by having the extra time to hold on to our cash. We count the material at the end of each month, let them know how much we used, and then they send us an invoice that we pay in 30 days. In essence, we are getting 30- to 60-day terms with an average of 45 days. Since our customers pay within an average of 47 days, it means that we don't end up carrying any inventory.

Ask if they will consider extended terms. Though early pay and consignment terms are better, this is an option if the supplier won't agree to them. In an informal conversation with your sales rep, ask how long you can go without paying until the rep starts to hear from the accounting department about the invoice. Be straightforward with the rep; explain that you're trying to be as financially efficient as possible. The rep may tell you that the official rule of thumb is 30 days but that they rarely if ever do anything until it reaches 60 or even 90 days. I'm not advising you to wait this amount of time to pay all your materials suppliers but simply to recognize that this may be a bargaining chip. One of the company owners I talked to told me that as a supplier to a number of companies with cash-flow problems, he offers 90-day payment terms because he knows he can't compete on price. In this way, his 90-day policy becomes a competitive advantage. If you have a supplier like this, you should explore the possibility of extended terms.

SCRAPPY COMPANIES

Because materials costs are often a company's biggest expense, you should do everything possible to obtain the best yield possible. For many companies, the scrap material is worth much less than the company originally paid for it, and at least some small businesses end up paying to have waste material hauled away. Let me suggest another way of dealing with scrap.

Jerry, the head of a small manufacturing operation, for years viewed scrap as an expense—they paid a significant amount of money annually to have someone take it off their hands. Finally, one of his vice presidents wondered during an executive meeting whether a use for the by-product material existed. They investigated and discovered a use, and they eventually made as much money from this by-product as their main product line. Even if your by-product seems worthless at first glance, it might be worth having a brainstorming session or bringing in a knowledgeable consultant to explore ways to make money from it. Every business is different, and finding ways to increase your material yields will vary from how another company in some other field would do it.

Howard Smith is the owner of Wilson Bohannon Lock Company, a manufacturer of industrial locks. They make their locks from brass bars, an extremely costly material. When I went to visit the company's manufacturing facility, I noticed that a person was manually cutting off short pieces of brass to make additional starting parts for locks. This struck me as odd, since it's an automated facility—you don't usually see people performing this type of manual task in a highly automated factory. Howard explained that their automated machines could not hold on to the very end of the bars, resulting in unusable bar ends that would be sold as scrap material. One day Howard was walking through the facility and saw a machine operator taking one of the bar ends and cutting one extra lock body from a bar end. It struck Howard that if the company made this a routine practice, it would save thousands of dollars annually in material cost.

You probably have ways to make relatively small adjustments in your own business that will result in big savings. To take advantage of these opportunities, however, you must be looking for them continuously. When it comes to manufacturing, a minor physical adjustment to a process or machine might do the trick. You should also be alert to more subtle opportunities. For example, our nesting software—software that helps you maximize usage of a given material—helped us reduce our raw material requirements by as much as 15 percent and also accelerated our programming speed.

MANUFACTURING CAPACITY: MAKING IT BIGGER WITHOUT TAKING ON MORE PEOPLE OR MACHINES

This is a dicey subject for a book on saving money. Traditionally, increasing capacity means making major investments in machinery. If your sales are great and you are running at 100 percent capacity, hiring more employees and building or expanding a plant is the logical next step. It is also a financially risky step, since as just about every small business owner knows, product demand is highly unpredictable. You can have a great month that would seem to be a harbinger of a great year, and then suddenly you lose a major customer or some other calamity strikes. In the '90s, many small companies expanded their capacity like crazy and then were severely crippled or put out of business when the downturn hit.

Clearly, you should not be idle when demand for your product skyrockets; you don't want to lose sales to competitors. At the same time, you don't want to risk your business on an expansion that might not be needed one year or even one month from now. Following are some cost-effective methods to expand capacity.

Subcontracting out some business. Many small business owners worry that the subcontractor won't do a good job and the company will alienate or lose customers, or that whatever money is earned from subcontracting won't be nearly as much as the company would make if it had the capacity to do the work in-house. These are reasonable concerns, but you may be able to alleviate them if you have a good subcontracting process.

First, don't subcontract routinely. It's a measure to be employed only when you either have to make a huge investment to expand or you'll lose the business.

Second, target certain types of jobs for subcontracting. The ideal job is one that you know is going to tie up your equipment for prolonged periods of time. These are the ones you want out of your system and in someone else's.

Third, use local contractors whom you know and trust. This means you can't wait until the last second to start searching for suitable companies to whom you'll give the work. You need to spend some time researching and meeting other companies in your area and establishing a relationship with them.

Fourth, determine a reasonable markup for the work—reasonable for you, for the subcontractor, and for your customer. Yes, prices are going to be high. Most of your customers, however, will accept the higher cost because these situations usually occur in strong economies. When you need greater capacity, your customers will also be doing well and will be more concerned about delivery than about price. During one year, we subcontracted over $180,000 in business with a 20 percent margin, adding $45,000 to our bottom line without incurring any debt, additional employees, or new equipment.

Explore used equipment purchases instead of new. This measure may be one you've considered only briefly or not at all; used equipment may cause more problems than it's worth, and it's tough to determine if you're getting a good deal.

However, I attended an equipment auction a few hours away from our plant that was offering an unusually good selection of only slightly used equipment. In fact, some of the equipment seemed as if it had hardly been used at all. It turned out that the owner of the business had bought around $2 million worth of equipment a few years previously, including a laser with a dual pallet changer and powder-coating line. Business was great at the time, and the owner was certain that the company would need all the additional capacity this equipment provided. Less than two years later, however, the market took a sharp downturn. The company couldn't afford the debt service from its capital investments; it had to sell and sell fast.

Whether you're going through ads in trade publications, Web sites, equipment brokers, or auctions, used equipment opportunities abound. If you really believe you need greater capacity to fuel growth, consider buying used instead of new—at least for some of your equipment needs. In addition, consider buying during a down cycle rather than when the economy is booming. In the previous example, the company paid top dollar for the equipment because demand was high. They sold at a much lower price because demand was lower. View down cycles as your window to get great deals on equipment, especially if it's used.

You should also look at the possibility of refurbishing equipment. Obviously, the more work it needs, the lower the purchase price. One small business owner I talked to told me that he buys only used equipment that needs to be refurbished. He estimates that even after paying for repairs, his purchases cost him about

40 percent less than the price of new equipment. Of course, this value can vary considerably depending on factors such as the age of the equipment, the hours of use accumulated, and refurbishing requirements.

Challenge yourself to increase capacity 10 percent without spending one additional dollar. At first, this may appear nonsensical: if you could increase capacity without spending money, you would already have done it. In reality, most of us aren't very creative when it comes to these types of exercises. Aside from asking people to work harder, what other possibilities are there? Here are some tactics that small companies have found to be effective.

First, experiment with running equipment during transitional periods. Most of you may be saying to yourself that you run your equipment steadily over three shifts, but what about the time between shifts: lunch periods, employee breaks, and shift changes?

When our company's capacity was being stretched to the limit, we realized that even though the machinery our employees operated was automatic, they put the machines on hold for the 20 minutes in which they ate lunch. This meant we were losing not only 20 minutes but 5 minutes to shut it down before lunch and 5 minutes to start it up when they returned. Multiplying this by three shifts, we saw that we were losing 1.5 hours daily. If we could find a way to use this time, we could increase capacity by 6.25 percent.

We began staggering employee lunches from nonmanufacturing departments to monitoring operating equipment when the manufacturing people were having lunch. While we had to do a bit of training, it wasn't much since monitoring the equipment was relatively easy. With almost no expenditures, we increased capacity by 6.25 percent.

A second option is move to a four-shift operation in which your equipment is running 24 hours a day, seven days a week. This isn't feasible for everyone; employees of many companies with older workforces, for example, don't like the notion of this untraditional schedule. A younger workforce, on the other hand, may be very receptive to four shifts because it gives them a few four- or even five-day weekends monthly, based on how the shifts are configured. Running four shifts requires a small investment—perhaps hiring three or four more people—but that's nothing when compared to the huge increase in capacity, usually about 14 percent. In addition, having a four-shift schedule means you don't have to worry about paying overtime for weekend work, since every day is a workday under the four-shift schedule.

Videotape your manufacturing department at work to determine the optimum work methods. Here's a truism that is often forgotten in the heat of the workday: every piece of equipment has an optimum setup and running procedure, but these procedures are often ignored. Certain operating techniques can minimize downtime and maximize output for any given piece of machinery; however, when equipment is five years old (or older), the people who know the secrets may have left the company, or it may be that one operator is following the right procedures while all the other operators are following less efficient ones.

Videotaping allows you to view operators in action and determine which ones are the most effective. It becomes a teaching tool for all the operators to learn where they aren't being as efficient as possible and techniques that will increase their productivity. It may not always yield results, but a few hours of videotape can give you valuable perspective on what procedures are being used and how they might be improved.

Give supervisors the right incentives. When overtime is required, make it a policy that one of your supervisors must be present to direct the workforce. This supervisor should not receive additional pay for coming in on the weekend; it is merely a policy you establish. At the same time, you should pay supervisors a bonus if they are able to reduce premium labor costs in relation to sales dollars annually.

These two tactics will encourage your supervisors to come up with ways to increase productivity during the week without having to come in on weekends. To measure whether your supervisors are meeting this goal, compare monthly or annual premium labor costs and measure this number as a percentage of sales dollars.

COMPARE, CONTRAST, LEARN

These three directives are the cornerstone of cost-effective manufacturing. However, small business owners sometimes become set in their ways and are unwilling or unable to disturb traditional manufacturing processes that have been in place for years. Knowledge is financial power, especially when it comes to manufacturing processes. Process and tooling technologies are changing so rapidly that what is cost-effective today may not be cost-effective tomorrow.

You need to make a commitment to learning. More specifically, you need to be open to new information and ideas about your manufacturing efficiency and effectiveness. You can test your openness to change by answering the following questions:

1. **Do you evaluate each process in your plant every three years?** This is the minimum necessary to keep up with technological developments.
2. **Do you visit at least five other facilities each year to determine what processes they are using and how these processes compare to your own?** These facilities can be in your area and industry, or they might be in other areas and other industries. The key is to make this effort and observe what other companies are doing that you might be able to adapt and apply in your plant.

3. **Do you encourage other small manufacturers to visit your facility?** Again, some small business owners are concerned about competition and don't want a rival stealing their great processes. Others are merely defensive and don't want to hear that another company is doing something differently or better. You'll find, however, that allowing visits from other business owners is like having an unpaid consultant. They come into your facility without any biases about your particular operation; they can look at it objectively and ask questions that you may not be asking because you're too close to what's going on.

4. **Do you ask your operators good questions, and do they feel free to respond honestly?** This give-and-take between you and the people who are closest to the equipment is crucial. If you ask perfunctory questions or no questions at all, you'll never learn what they know. If they feel you don't really want honest responses, you'll also be in the dark. Your operators know the nuances of the machines they operate, and by communicating with you about their concerns and questions, they give you a way to save money.

For instance, one of my operators recently asked me why we carried two different sizes of grinding wheels, since our grinding machines were all similar. I wasn't quite sure what the answer to the question was, so I asked around and discovered that one machine had a hub that was different from the hubs on all the others—our other machines had been modified and this one hadn't. As a result, certain types of grinding wheels came with this machine, and the purchasing department had simply bought the same type of replacement wheels and never questioned why they were different. It turned out that it would take our staff about two hours to modify this machine's hub so that it was like all the others, and we could then buy just one type of grinding wheel. This small modification saved us about $1,000 annually. More significantly, it taught me that there are many of these opportunities for incremental savings, but you have to ask questions of the people on the line to find out what they are.

5. **Do you have a state-of-the-art tooling expert?** Tooling changes with astonishing speed, and if you don't have an expert who can help you upgrade your tooling, you'll lose money through inefficiency and lost productivity. Finding a tooling sage isn't easy, but every small manufacturer should make it a priority.

   We have traditionally purchased right-handed flute reamers for our hole finishing. Based on our expert's suggestion, we are now in the process of changing them to left-handed flutes. This has improved the life of the reamers and the finish of the holes. With a longer life span, less resharpening of the tooling is needed. While our initial cost was high for these new reamers, we project a 15 to 20 percent gain in productivity. We needed an expert in this instance because we lacked an employee who knew the benefit we'd receive from left-handed reamers, and our expert's suggestion made this significant gain possible.

6. **Are you willing to automate, and are you actively looking for automation opportunities?** This question is relevant now more than ever. If you don't start automating now, you'll regret it later. Yes, automation requires a financial investment, but this expenditure is nothing compared to rising labor costs. Small business owners tend to be myopic when it comes to decisions that involve a choice between machines and people. They assume that it's cheaper to use people than to buy expensive machinery. What they don't realize is that we are burdened with an aging labor force, and that labor shortages in most industries will be inevitable in the near future.

   Therefore, you should at least evaluate what operations can be automated and how the costs for doing so would compare to the current and projected costs of people doing these same jobs. Obviously, some jobs are still done more effectively by people than by machines, so the idea is not to get rid of as many people as you can as fast as you can. Instead, be continuously aware of automation possibilities and don't be afraid to make the transition from people to automation when it is warranted.

10

CAPITAL INVESTMENTS VERSUS CAPITAL PUNISHMENT

Whether you're a manufacturer or a service provider, you need to buy different types of equipment at certain points in time. Obviously, manufacturers have to make much greater equipment investments, but most companies end up purchasing supplies such as computers, copiers, shredders, videoconferencing systems, and phone systems.

Large organizations generally have a sophisticated process in place and expert purchasing managers in charge to ensure the best deal possible. The company weighs its options, considers various suppliers, looks at the pros and cons of leasing versus buying, and determines if it really needs to replace a piece of equipment immediately or ever.

Small businesses tend to make these decisions impulsively or through an informal, inefficient process. As a result, they frequently overpay, buy unnecessary equipment, and ignore cost-saving options. They also convince themselves that they've done due diligence before making a purchase, but what they've really done is marginal diligence; they asked the manufacturing head if a new machine is really necessary or if replacing the broken part would be sufficient.

When it comes to saving money on equipment, you need to ask a lot of questions. First, though, you should set up some simple but often overlooked screening procedures for new purchases.

WILL YOUR PURCHASE SIT IN A BOX AND GATHER DUST?

Cost-justifying significant expenditures seems like an obvious part of the process, but when you're operating under great pressure and dealing with one crisis after the next, cost justification often slips through the cracks. When a piece of equipment breaks down, work grinds to a halt, and each second of down time represents many dollars lost; you want to get that piece of equipment up and running as fast as possible. Consequently, you may spend more than you should for the sake of speed.

While I recognize that many business owners often lack the luxury of time to do research and shop around before making a purchase, a window of opportunity usually exists to justify expenditure. To take advantage of this window, take three simple actions right from the start that will tell you whether the purchase is worth it.

1. Subject a prospective capital expenditure to the box test. When I became the owner of my current company, I was familiarizing myself with the factory and came across a piece of equipment that had been sitting in a crate at the plant for three months. The equipment, bought by the previous owners, had cost $40,000. Though I quickly had our staff unpack the crate and install the equipment, the experience taught me that before making a major expenditure such as this one, you need to ask yourself the following question:

Will our purchase sit around in a box for months gathering dust before we get around to using it?

Most small companies can't afford to make major capital expenditures and not take advantage of them immediately. Just-in-time purchasing is generally the way to go for small companies. If your answer to the previous question is that it might sit around gathering dust for a while, then you should probably hold off on making the purchase until you're sure you can use it.

2. Conduct a return on investment (ROI) analysis. This may be something that you already do, but then you rationalize the results and make the purchase regardless of what the ROI reveals. As a general rule, you should be wary of any purchase that won't pay for itself within three or four years. This may seem like a short time frame, but most small businesses can't afford to make too many capital investments that don't have a relatively quick ROI.

Be especially wary of purchasing the latest, greatest technological improvement. In these days of seemingly daily technological breakthroughs, it is all too easy to convince yourself that you must have the newest model that is incrementally faster, more durable, or more multifaceted. We all are seduced by new technologies and by the knowledge that at some point in the future, these technologies will be critical to our business. If the future is ten years down the road, however, you may not need to spend $50,000 this year so that your machines run 2 percent faster.

3. Talk to at least three different manufacturers before making a buying decision. You may have a preferred supplier or be offered a deal that seems terrific. Nonetheless, spend the extra time to contact two other suppliers. By doing so, you have a basis for comparison that can save you money. Many times, small business owners jump at what seems to be an unbeatable price. In fact, the low price may be on the level, but all sorts of hidden costs may come with that price; the service agreement may be mediocre, or the quality of certain parts may be below standard.

In this area, as in others, knowledge saves you money. By making the effort to consult with three different suppliers, you'll probably gain valuable information that you would be less likely to learn if you confined your conversation to one supplier. Invariably, you'll discover a trick to getting the most out of a piece of equipment or a tip that, although the current machinery is good, a new generation of machine that will be released next year represents a quantum leap in quality.

TWENTY QUESTIONS: WHAT YOU NEED TO ASK AND HOW TO INTERPRET THE ANSWERS

Let's assume you've talked to three different manufacturers, your ROI is good, and the purchase passes the box test. No doubt, after your prospective capital investment has run this gauntlet, you're ready to make the buy. Before doing so, you should take the time to answer 20 questions. It may be that some of these questions aren't relevant for a given purchase or you already know the answers, so you can skip the unnecessary ones and focus on the others. In fact, you may have limited time to buy and excellent knowledge related to a given capital investment, and you don't want to go through the process of asking these questions. In this instance, it's still a good idea to review the questions relevant to a given purchase and see if any of them raise red flags in your mind. If so, then you should definitely seek out the answers before buying.

Now let's turn to the questions:

1. **How long has the seller's company been around?** Yes, some companies are not to be trusted even though they've been around for a long time. Still, I would be wary of any brand-new manufacturer. If the owners have a track record with

a previous company, that's good, but if they have relatively little experience, then that's at least a yellow flag. A number of small business owners related stories about buying an expensive piece of equipment that broke down at some point, and when they tried to get in touch with the seller, the company had vanished from the face of the earth: their warranty was worthless, no one had the part they needed, and it was difficult to find anyone with the expertise to repair the specific piece of equipment.

2. **How long has the company been making a particular piece of equipment?** Cutting-edge technology is great, but if a machine is in its first year, it may have quality problems or other glitches that haven't yet been discovered. This is similar to the old adage about buying a car in its first model year: let other people be plagued with first-year problems and wait to buy the product until these issues have been fixed. If a company has been making a specific product for three years or more, then the odds are that they've corrected whatever problems customers complained about when it was first launched.

3. **Are parts readily available?** Don't assume that parts are easily obtainable. You may discover that it's not only difficult but also expensive to obtain replacement parts. What you want to know is what parts are most commonly replaced, how long it takes to obtain them, and what the costs are.

4. **Are the replacement parts standard or custom?** Custom parts typically have long lead times and are more expensive than standard parts. You want to buy a piece of equipment that has as few custom replacement parts as possible. Let's say that Machine Manufacturer A has a press that is equipped with a hydraulic cylinder available from any parts supplier, and Machine Manufacturer B has a hydraulic cylinder that is custom-made by the machine manufacturer. If the machines are comparable in their capabilities, the

financially astute decision would be to go with A because of the superior availability, and probably the lower cost, of replacement parts.

5. **How many service technicians does your supplier employ?** Contrary to what you might think, more is not always better. If a company tells you they have a large staff of service technicians, this may indicate that the company's machines have so many service problems that many technicians are necessary. At the same time, if they have one person whose phone is always busy and who never is available to schedule a meeting, that should also be cause for concern. Ideally, a company will have a moderate number of technicians.

6. **What is the service technician turnover rate?** Of course, companies with a high turnover rate may not admit to this fact. If you've bought products from the manufacturer in the past and found that the service technician you talked to was gone the next month, or other companies have bought from this supplier and tell you that they never have the same technician twice, then that is a sign you should heed. It takes most technicians a certain amount of time to familiarize themselves with a particular company's equipment quirks. They must go through a trial-and-error process before they're skilled at diagnosing and fixing equipment problems, and a technician who has some experience with the company is more likely to be invested in doing a thorough job.

7. **Where are the technicians located?** If the company's technicians are so far away that they need to be flown in to solve problems, this can cost you money both directly and indirectly. Directly, the company is going to charge more if it needs to bring in technicians from thousands of miles away. Indirectly, you'll end up paying for the lack of timely service—getting someone to travel from across the country or another country will prevent you from having your

equipment up and running quickly, and the downtime will be costly.

8. **How many machines have been sold, and can they supply references?** A company that has sold a significant number of machines generally has done so for a good reason. These machines could be more reliable, faster, of higher quality, or very well priced. It is always good to obtain references; it's even better to obtain a reference that the salesperson has not provided you. You might also ask the salesperson for a list of the last four or five companies that have bought a machine. If these companies are not competitors, call them yourself and try to learn what you can from them.

9. **What type of computer controls does the machine have?** You want something that is user-friendly, and you want to avoid having to bring in a highly trained programmer to operate the equipment. You want the average user to be able to pick up the programming of the machine and understand what it takes to make changes to a program. You also want to strive for compatibility with other software. For example, our business software allows us to create reports, download this same information easily into Excel, and create very useful summary reports that help us make important decisions in operating our business.

10. **What type of regular preventative maintenance does the manufacturer recommend?** One small business owner I know was considering switching suppliers because a competing supplier guaranteed that new equipment would run almost twice as fast as what the company was currently using. This guarantee was a powerful incentive to switch, since increasing production was a key goal for the company and this supplier seemed to be offering a way to reach this goal. By asking this particular question, however, the small business owner discovered that speed came

at a steep cost. The new equipment was so temperamental that it required a significant investment in preventative maintenance—an investment that wasn't worth it no matter how much speed was gained.

11. **How long does it take to set up each machine?** New equipment might run three times faster than your current system, but if it also takes four times longer to set up the next job, it doesn't take a rocket scientist to tell you that this is not a beneficial change. You make money only when the machine is running, so maximizing its operating time is paramount. The setup needs to be simple and fast.

12. **How much time does it take to train an operator?** Some equipment is challenging for new users. As a result, you incur unforeseen costs in helping employees learn how to operate machines effectively. It's one thing if it takes a few days before someone has mastered the equipment's operation. It's something else entirely if weeks or even months pass before the operator has figured out all of a new machine's idiosyncrasies. A consultant may be helpful in facilitating training. Even if this isn't necessary, you still lose money if training drags on, preventing the efficient use of the new equipment for an extended period.

13. **What skill level does an operator need?** Some equipment requires enormous amounts of experience and talent, while other equipment can be operated effectively by most employees. Figure out whether a prospective purchase is closer to the former or the latter type.

14. **What skill level do the maintenance personnel need?** If machinery demands a lot of care and feeding, you could end up spending more than you had anticipated. Will you need to send your staff to the manufacturer's facility to learn how to maintain the machine, or can they be trained on-site at your facility? Will they need special tooling to do the maintenance on the machine?

15. **What type of power hookup does the equipment require?** Small business owners often overlook this simple question when making a purchase. Some buildings have been added onto at various points in time, and the power coming into these additions is not always the same. Older buildings are often equipped with 240 V, while newer buildings all have 480 V, which is more efficient. If you haven't done your homework, you end up having to buy a step-up or a step-down transformer to get the proper power to the machine. This can be an expensive mistake. One business owner had to spend an extra $10,000 for a transformer and an extra day for the electrical contractor because of this type of oversight.

16. **How much will it cost to power this machine each year?** The machine manufacturer should be able to tell you what the cost to operate the machine each year will be or provide a close approximation. If you are buying used equipment, obtain the information from the identification plate on the machine. It should tell you how many amperes the machine will draw and what voltage is required. Given this information and your cost of electricity per kilowatt hour, an electrician can calculate the approximate cost to operate a piece of equipment.

17. **How long does the manufacturer plan to keep making the piece of equipment you're purchasing?** Of course, they may tell you that they're going to make it for the next 100 years, while in reality they're already planning its replacement. Ideally, suppliers will be honest with you, since it's in their best interest to keep you as a customer. They should tell you that you have the option of waiting for a year to purchase the next generation of machine or of purchasing this one now at a sizable discount. It's also a good idea to network within your industry and read your trade publications, since word may leak that the

machine you're planning on purchasing will be phased out soon.

18. **What type of warranty comes with the machine?** A minimum of a one-year warranty is necessary. You may be aware of the axiom that if a new car is a lemon, you'll discover this fact during the first year. The same principle holds true for most types of machines.

19. **Can you buy an extended warranty?** You always want to push the envelope as far as you can. If you can convince the manufacturer to extend the warranty for additional time, take it. It's a negotiating point. If you have an equipment supplier who won't budge on the price, try to bargain for an extended warranty.

20. **What kind of lead time do they promise once the equipment is ordered?** More to the point, what is their delivery guarantee, if any? One small manufacturing company received the largest order in its history, and it recognized that it had to make a capital investment to meet the continuing requirements of this new customer. The owner considered all of the issues and questions discussed here—except for this one. As a result, the company waited with increasing frustration and anger as delivery was delayed for six weeks. During that time, the owner threatened and begged to no avail. The supplier made all sorts of excuses, but whether these excuses were legitimate is beside the point. This small business owner never asked about lead time or delivery guarantee, and this essentially let the manufacturer off the hook. The small business was fortunate enough not to lose its large new customer, but the owner did have to offer a number of discounts to that customer to make up for the delay.

WHAT TO ASK FOR: NEGOTIATE YOUR WAY TO A BETTER INVESTMENT

After you've asked your 20 questions, you should also ask for 12 different things from a supplier that may make even good capital investments more cost-effective. Don't be satisfied with a good piece of equipment at a fair price. In certain situations, you can and should expect more. You may be looking to buy during a buyer's market. You may not realize that a given supplier has a surplus of the equipment you want to purchase and is willing to bend over backward to find more buyers. A supplier may see you as a potential long-term customer and may be open to providing various perks to establish a strong relationship.

Whatever the reason, negotiate by asking for one or more of the following:

- **Extended terms.** For instance, request six months before your first payment is due. If you're strapped for cash when you must make a major capital investment, which is not an unusual circumstance for many small business owners, this extension will ease the financial pressure during a critical period. If you're going to finance your purchase, talk to the seller about financing terms. A number of small business owners fail to do this, assuming that their banks will offer the best rates. This isn't always true. Some equipment suppliers have their own finance companies, and in certain instances, their terms are more favorable than those of your local bank. The availability of favorable financing helps them to sell more equipment.
- **Extended service contract.** Asking for an additional year may not seem like much, but it's often that additional year that's not covered when something seems to go wrong. Potentially, this can save you a significant amount of money,

and this small concession is something many sellers are willing to make to get your business.

- **Additional training for operators and maintenance staff.** A typical week of training can cost $1,500 or more. If your employees don't have a lot of experience with a given piece of equipment or system, this can be a major cost-saving benefit. It's also a logical one to negotiate for; sellers can understand why it should be part of the package and may provide it without hesitation, especially if you're buying new or complex equipment. If your purchase is a new phone system, I'd highly recommend negotiating for training, since some new phone systems are notoriously difficult to master for small businesses.

- **Additional tooling or supplies that aren't normally included.** As you certainly know, every capital investment carries additional costs beyond the stated price. If your purchase is for a significant amount of money, you might request that a few extra items be thrown into the deal.

- **Additional spare parts that might be perishable.** Typically, all equipment has some parts that are going to wear out. Maybe it is a belt that drives the motor, special grease, a spare motor, or an extra clamping fixture. One business owner asked for all of these items with the purchase of a new grinder. He knew that these were key parts to have after talking with someone else who had purchased the same machine a year earlier.

- **Free machine upgrades.** Maybe the machine has additional capabilities that are not necessary based on the products you produce today, but they could be something you would consider in the future, or maybe they increase resale value of the machine when you want to sell it. Upgrades might include extra guarding; ability to machine bigger, smaller, thicker, or thinner parts; ability to machine in another axis (move in another direction); or a bigger monitor with a computer. Again, this can be an effective bargaining point if the seller won't move on price.

- **Additional memory for machines.** For example, one business owner negotiated for extra memory for his laser so that he could load bigger programs in the machine. This allowed him to load longer-running jobs on the machine and operate more efficiently. This would also have been a value upon resale of the machine down the road. Every time we buy a new server for our business, the seller tells me we are getting so much memory that we will never need all of it. Then in four years, we are upgrading again because we used up all the memory they told us we would never use. More always seems to be better, so take it if you can get it.

- **Generate programs in advance that are part of the purchase price.** This shortens the learning curve for your programmers and allows you to hit the ground running as soon as the equipment is installed. Most businesses have some standard items that they make daily. Get the programs to run these parts made ahead of time.

- **Technicians available during installation.** While this isn't a big expense on the supplier's part, it can help you maximize your return on investment faster. No matter how skilled your employees are, they can't match the inside knowledge of the supplier's technical staff. Having them there during installation to install equipment properly and train your employees can help you avoid the costly start-up mistakes that are all too common.

- **A performance agreement.** This agreement could be for a specified productivity level or other measures. Many times, sellers promise that a piece of equipment will perform at a certain speed or handle a certain capacity, and all you're asking them to do is back up that claim with a guarantee.

- **Faster delivery.** As we've seen, slow delivery can cause huge problems for companies that can't afford delays. If you know that you need a given system or machine to be up and running immediately or you're liable to lose significant dollars (or fail to capitalize on a money-making opportunity), then negotiate better delivery terms than a manufacturer's standard agreement.

11

PURCHASING EVERYTHING FROM CLEANING SERVICES TO COFFEE

Though we examined cost-saving purchasing approaches for equipment earlier, I want to broaden the topic to all types of purchases here. Purchasing always offers potential opportunities for saving money. This may seem counterintuitive (if you're buying, how can you be saving?), but it makes sense when you realize you need to make a certain number of purchases as the cost of doing business. There's no way around this, even for the most frugal CEO in the world. At the same time, if you think about purchasing as a flexible activity with a range of options, you realize that it involves more than just paying the sticker price.

Many small business owners are ingenious when it comes to purchasing. After all, small companies probably make hundreds, if not thousands, of purchases annually. While some are for small amounts, many are for significant sums of money. Let's say a typical business makes 1,000 separate purchases annually of products and services, with each transaction averaging $100. Let's further assume that you can save an average of 5 percent, or $5 per transaction. That would mean that your total annual savings would be $5,000!

In reality, saving 5 percent per transaction is a modest objective. Simply making the effort to comparison shop with some regularity should yield a 5 percent purchasing reduction. I believe, however, that many businesses can reach a 10 percent reduction goal by using the tools and techniques in this chapter. Before offering you some tactics to achieve this goal, I'd like to share an instructive pair of stories with you.

THE LAMP AND COUCH LESSON

A couple stopped at a furniture store to look for a lamp for their living room. They found one they really liked for $75. They decided not to buy it, though, because they knew that another store just down the road carried the same line of furniture, and they thought they might find it there at a better price. They arrived at the second store and found the same lamp they liked from the first store, but its price was $100. The couple decided that they really liked the lamp and that they would buy it.

Now, ask yourself: What would you do in this couple's place? Would you go back to the first store and buy the $75 lamp? Most small business owners would probably agree that this would be the logical course of action.

A few weeks later, this same couple is looking for a couch, and they find one they love for $1,500. Again, they decide to shop around and find the same couch at another store for $1,525.

If you were this couple, would you travel back to the first store to save $25? My guess is that most small business owners would not, probably reasoning, "It's only $25 more."

In reality, that $25 should be just as important to the couple as it was when they were buying the lamp. Small business owners, however, sometimes adopt the "it's just $25 more" mentality for big-ticket items. If you want to save money, though, you will make a practice of comparison shopping and, when all other things are equal, taking the lowest price. As you'll see, that $25 often adds up to thousands of dollars over the course of purchases throughout a year.

HIRE A PURCHASING MANAGER WHO KNOWS AND DRIVES A GOOD BARGAIN

Many small companies have efficient purchasing managers, but they may not have highly effective ones, at least when it comes to cost consciousness. When I interview other small company CEOs about their purchasing managers, they usually say that the purchasing heads "know their stuff" and have established good relationships with vendors. When I ask if they show a talent for negotiating great deals or creativity when it comes to making purchases that pay off in the long term (rather than meeting only a short-term need), they often look at me blankly. The job description for a purchasing manager often doesn't include these attributes.

Therefore, start out with a list of the following extra credit qualifications the next time a position opens in your purchasing department:

____ Derives a sense of accomplishment from negotiating a better deal than the previous one.

____ Has a track record of finding ways to cut costs across the board.

____ Is astute about how far to push suppliers in terms of price and does so without being unfair or obnoxious.

____ Is willing to shop around for better deals, even though this requires a greater investment of time and effort.

____ Networks well and often finds bargains and superior suppliers through this network.

_____ Has good judgment about when it's cost-effective to pay more in the short term for a high-quality, longer-lasting product.

_____ Can evaluate service providers not just on the basis of price but on the value they add through trustworthiness, commitment, and other intangibles.

_____ Is able to differentiate something that's cheap from something that is a good bargain.

_____ Evaluates suppliers continuously rather than finding a good one and sticking with it, no questions asked.

_____ Makes sure inventory on critical supplies doesn't run low and is proactive about ordering in advance so that there are no premium charges for emergency purchases.

Here's a story that illustrates why the previous checklist is important when both hiring and measuring the performance of a purchasing manager. Larry had been the top purchasing executive for a small manufacturing company for 15 years. He always received above-average rankings on performance reviews and got along well with everyone. The company's new owner, Marie, bought the company about two years ago and was troubled by certain peculiarities about how the department functioned. For one thing, Larry reported to the controller, which struck Marie as odd. The controller knew relatively little about purchasing and thus could not really hold Larry accountable. Second, Marie found that every so often, shortages occurred in raw materials or the company ran out of tooling, and Larry didn't have a good explanation of why these things happened beyond "That's just the nature of purchasing." Third, one of the company's manufacturing managers ordered replacement parts and other materials on her own rather than go through purchasing, claiming that it was easier for her to do it on her own.

Marie decided that Larry might do a better job if she became Larry's supervisor. Within a few months, however, Larry decided to leave the company, claiming it was too stressful having Marie as his boss. Using the criteria in the checklist, Marie hired a new purchasing manager, and the change in purchasing cost-effectiveness was immediately apparent. No longer were there costly shortages of materials. All purchasing became centralized and highly efficient; no manager in any department was making significant purchases without going through the purchasing manager. Perhaps most significantly, Marie found that the new purchasing manager cared enough to find ways to drive purchasing costs down, whether through reassessing suppliers or negotiating new and improved deals with current suppliers.

Another recommendation from small business owners is that you set up a bonus program to motivate the purchasing manager to meet objectives. Here, you should set the bar high initially for purchasing managers: to receive the bonus, they must save 1.5 times their salary through wise purchasing decisions and policies. Create a centralized system to monitor and record monthly savings.

When we implemented this incentive program, our purchasing manager generated a $75,000 cost savings in the first year! He helped reduced our raw material costs through bargaining and comparison shopping, and he also instituted a policy of buying material closer to the finish thickness we needed; this minimized the extra machining necessary to make parts that fit our customers' requirements.

Obviously, to meet or beat objectives in the second year requires a certain amount of ingenuity—once you've made certain changes in purchasing strategy, you've already cut the most obvious costs. Our purchasing manager, in his second year of this incentive program, called each and every one of our suppliers and asked if they would offer early payment terms, requesting that if we pay within ten days, we receive a discount. This whole process of negotiating payment terms is really a three-step process. First, the purchasing agent needs to negotiate the best possible price from the suppliers, asking for discount terms. Many suppliers appreciate getting their money quickly from their customers. Cash flow is critical, and they will offer discounts if you pay your bills in ten days or less rather than the typical 30-day terms. Negotiate your best price first, and then ask if the supplier offers discounts for early payment terms. This is something that most salespeople will not present to you, so you have to ask. Typically, the salesperson wants the sale and is not going to protest these terms. As I mentioned earlier in Chapter 9, we saved $22,000 in 2005 by taking advantage of discounts.

Second, ask if they accept credit card payments. If you can get a supplier to give you early payment discounts and allow you to pay by credit card, you are being financially savvy. If you are turned down on your request for early payment discounts, use the credit card request as a bargaining tool. If the seller agrees to this, you receive an extra 30 days to pay and as much as 45 days if you time it right. You also receive points that can be applied to your card's reward program. Last year we accumulated 375,000 points on our credit card. At 30,000 to 35,000 points per airline ticket, that's ten free flights per year.

Finally, if the supplier does not offer discounted terms and will not accept credit card payments, then request 60-day terms to pay your bills rather than the normal 30-day terms. The extra 30 days beyond normal terms is extremely helpful in improving your business cash flow. Lack of proper cash flow is one of the major factors in business failure today. Extended payment terms are especially helpful in businesses that are just starting out or in a growth mode or those that have expensive inventory.

THINK OUTSIDE THE BOX, CRATE, AND CARTON

Purchases come in all shapes, sizes, and containers, and your approach to purchasing should be similarly wide-ranging. You must push yourself to think in different ways about how, when, and from whom you purchase. This requires a bit of time and effort. It also may require some tough conversations with suppliers and some tough decisions about whether to stay with them. The key, though, is not limiting your purchasing focus to one area or one issue. Every small business makes a huge number of purchases annually, and at least some of those purchases need to be examined in a fresh light.

To help you gain this fresh perspective, here are a wide range of actions you can take:

- **Put your shipping costs under the microscope.** You are dealing with a service that is in plentiful supply. Consequently, you have numerous options as well as significant bargaining power. Talk to other shippers about their prices; tell your current shipper if someone else offers you a better deal and see if they'll match it. Explore cost-saving shipping options, such as adding a day to the shipping time for a better price or using one form of transportation (truck) versus another (air). You might also want to investigate different shipping packages. By shopping around, we reduced our pallet cost by $1 per shipment, which translated into savings of $2,500 annually.

- **Evaluate what you're paying for yard work.** Many small companies have grounds that they must maintain. Generally, the two biggest costs in this regard are lawn care and snow removal. We know companies that have saved $5,000 or more annually by moving these functions in-house. They simply have their own employees mow and shovel. Another option is to use an outside service for this maintenance but have it come less frequently. You can also explore the option of hiring local kids to handle these tasks rather than a professional service.

- **Clean up without being wiped out.** Here is another area where the supply generally exceeds the demand. Office cleaning services charge fees that vary considerably, and while one cleaning service that charges a premium might do a better and faster job than another one, I would tend to go for the lowest-cost provider in this area. We reduced our office cleaning service by $720 annually by shopping around, and most other small companies can reduce their bills through comparing prices and bargaining.

- **Filter your coffee expenses.** I recognize that this isn't a big expense, but it's also an area where small companies waste money. In a time where there's a premium coffee retailer on every corner, employees are no longer dependent on a company providing a coffee machine and coffee for every department or work area. The odds are that a significant percentage of your employees prefer the coffee they buy at a local retailer. I'm not saying you have to eliminate your coffee service supplier, but you probably would save some money if you found a less expensive supplier or simply bought a few coffee machines and a generic brand of coffee.

- **Make negotiation a reflex.** You don't always have to pay list price, though in the United States, that assumption often governs most of our purchases. I know many small business owners and their purchasing managers don't like to negotiate price. They believe they are insulting suppliers when they tell them they're not going to pay one price but they would be willing to pay another. While it's true that some suppliers will refuse to negotiate, many others will. They will, that is, assuming your employees are willing to say no to paying list price.

To help encourage a negotiating reflex, here are some tips other small business owners have found to be effective:

- **Use the logic card.** Don't just say, "No, that price is too high." Suggest a solid reason why they should offer a lower price. For instance, your logic might be another supplier is offering the same product or service for less. Or your logic might be that you buy in bulk, so you should receive a volume discount. Encourage your employees to come up with a sound argument for requesting a lower price. This logic will make it easier for them to negotiate.

- **Use trade-offs.** To get something, you often have to give something in return. Encourage your employees to have a list of trades they might be willing to make to save money. For instance, they might be willing to provide the supplier's name to three prospective customers. Or they might be willing to accept a longer delivery time in exchange for a lower price. Like the logic card, thinking in trade-off terms facilitates negotiation.

- **Bring in a negotiation expert to talk to your employees.** This might be an investment worth making, especially if you find that your staff doesn't grasp how to negotiate. You'll find that certain consultants are very smart about negotiation tactics, and it might take as little as an hour or two for them to share useful techniques with your purchasing department.

- **Invoke the three-supplier rule.** This rule is simple: every so often, your purchasing department must contact two additional suppliers besides the one they regularly use, ask for bids, and compare prices and other elements. Your employees may do this for big-ticket items but mainly adhere to the one-supplier rule: they've already found a supplier they like and trust, and they feel it's a betrayal if they start shopping around for other suppliers. In reality, it's a betrayal only if they find another supplier for petty or personal reasons. If someone else is offering a better price, is trustworthy, and has faster service, it's good business to switch. Yes, contacting three suppliers instead of relying on one requires more time, but it's time well spent. Your goal should be not to motivate your employees to do this with every vendor every time they want to make a new purchase, but to shop around semiregularly to ensure that they're getting good deals.

CREDIT WHERE CREDIT IS DUE

I offer this suggestion cautiously, since it can be a surefire method to lose money rather than save it. Still, I urge you to obtain a credit card for your purchasing manager to use whenever possible. Most credit cards are linked to a cash-back or rewards program, and if you make a substantial number of purchases on the card in a given year, you will be able to save money directly or indirectly. We charge about $375,000 in credit card expenses annually, and last year we received ten free flights to anywhere in the United States as a result of the card's rewards program. You may want to use a card that will offer other rewards besides free flights, such as points toward the purchase price of a new vehicle, but you should consider a variety of card programs and figure out which one will best meet your needs.

If cash flow is a big issue in your business, credit cards may be useful if you use them judiciously. Bob Gase, my cousin, is the head of Gase Construction. In the construction business, the expenses required for building a home can often outweigh the draw a bank provides to complete different portions of the project. To deal with this potential cash-flow problem, Bob uses credit cards in certain situations. For instance, he typically receives at least 45 days to pay his bills using credit cards. As you probably know, credit card companies require payment in 30 days or they start charging interest. Bob, however, knows exactly when the billing periods start and end on each of his cards, so depending on where he is in a billing period, Bob times his purchases so that he receives the maximum amount of time before his credit card payment is due.

He always pays within the terms, makes sure he gets his reward points, and never incurs any interest expense.

Now the warning about credit cards: do not use credit cards for financing purposes. As you may know, card interest rates are very high—much higher than traditional bank loans or lines of credit. Pay off the full amount owed per card each month.

BE SAVVY BUT DON'T BE A BULLY

Saving the company money in the purchasing department isn't all about demanding the best prices you can get from suppliers. It's also about working smarter and spending your money more wisely. It's about finding alternatives. For instance, find a way to reduce the amount of inventory you need to keep for an item. One business owner recently hired a new purchasing manager who quickly found that the company was carrying over six months of inventory valued at approximately $100,000. After some investigation, the new purchasing manager found that most of the product they kept in inventory was standard material and could be purchased from local suppliers within a couple of days. Several years ago, obtaining this product had taken longer, but a new supplier that carried a broader inventory and could supply the product quickly had since come into the area. Within six months, the company reduced its inventory by over $70,000.

Another recent example of purchasing savvy happened in our office. We utilize a weekly throw rug delivery service, as do many businesses. But I doubt that many small business owners realize what it costs to have those things changed each week. I also doubt that many people know that they reproduce, or at least they seem to! If you start out with one or two, in a couple of months there will be three or four. Our purchasing manager was able to cut back on the number of rugs we use and saved us about $4,000 a year.

Finally, purchasing savvy often boils down to one part common sense and one part diligence. Phillip Clouse is the former purchasing director for Newel Rubbermaid, and he now works for a large, privately held company in a similar position. His story illustrates this purchasing formula.

His company was importing product from around the world, and when Phillip became involved, he realized that no one was monitoring the freight costs. Phillip took on the task of negotiating better terms with his company's carriers, and within 60 days, he had saved his company nearly $6 million! Phillip correctly rationalized that this was a fertile area for saving money because no one had been paying much attention to it, and this inattention probably was resulting in overpaying for freight. Because the company was spending a great deal of money on freight, reducing the company's costs by only 5 percent resulted in a savings of $6 million. Small reductions on big-ticket items are the easiest way for a purchasing manager to save a company big money.

12

HIDDEN OPPORTUNITIES: THE SAVINGS THAT EXIST BENEATH THE SURFACE

A small business owner has hundreds of opportunities daily to save money or spend money cost-effectively. Many times, these opportunities are invisible, hidden by the administrative routine. Small business executives go through the day and fall into a pattern of decision making. Even if they realize there is a chance to save money, they don't pay much attention to it because they're blinded by the routine: they've always done things one way, and it's difficult to consider changing. As a result, small adjustments aren't made and money isn't saved.

However, paying attention to these details will pay off, and there are ways to become aware of diverse hidden opportunities to reduce spending or cut costs. While I've touched on a few of these methods, I want to give you a better sense of where these opportunities lie and how you can take advantage of them. As you'll see, they involve everything from reducing paperwork to controlling computer supply costs.

TECH-RELATED OFFICE SUPPLIES

Many small businesses order printer toner cartridges as if they own significant blocks of stock in the cartridge manufacturers. They may exhibit the same buying behavior when it comes to copier paper and personal computers. Yes, a business needs all of these products to function. At the same time, there are ways to save when purchasing these items—options that are frequently ignored. Let's look at some alternatives that may exist beneath the radar:

- **Buy refurbished toner cartridges.** This requires a bit of a search, but just about every company has a computer geek on its payroll. This might not even be someone in your MIS department; it may be an individual who works on the loading dock or a financial executive who has spent years looking for the best deals on cartridges and other technological materials for personal use. Put this person in charge of finding a reputable source for refurbished toner cartridges. Finding a good source may save you hundreds to thousands of dollars annually.

- **Use both sides of copier and fax paper.** When you've used one side and are ready to use the other, just put an X over the used side. With this simple action, you've reduced your copier and fax paper costs by 50 percent and implemented an environmentally responsible policy. In addition, look into software that can automatically forward your faxes to your e-mail program. You can then open the fax on your computer screen and determine whether you really need to print a hard copy. Not only do you save paper, but you can also reduce the toner needed for your fax machine. It also allows people who are traveling to access their faxed messages faster. Rather than waiting until they return to the office to check their faxes, they can do so from anywhere as long as they can connect to the Internet.

- **Follow cost-conscious printer commands.** Printers are relatively inexpensive, so many small business owners end up buying more of them than the office really needs. They fail to consider how expensive replacing cartridges, even refurbished ones, can become. Be aware that not every workstation needs a dedicated printer; by networking computers together, you can reduce your printer purchases significantly. Buy color printers only when absolutely necessary—their cartridges are more expensive than black-and-white ones. Before making a printer purchase, evaluate its price against the price of its cartridges. In some instances, it makes sense to buy a more expensive printer with less expensive replacement cartridges, depending on how quickly you believe you'll go through cartridges.

ACCOUNTS PAYABLE INVOICES AND AGREEMENTS: A SLEW OF SAVINGS WAITING TO BE DISCOVERED

In most small businesses, at least one person reviews invoices and agreements to verify that you're being charged the right amount and that, if an invoice has been paid, this amount has been deducted from the remaining amount due. However, you can probably benefit from implementing a thorough system for reviewing these documents and ensuring that it is followed consistently. If you have a $5 million business, you might be able to save as much as $5,000 by reviewing these pieces of paper carefully.

Don't limit your review to the purchasing manager. Identify an employee who has a knack for spotting mistakes or identifying numbers that simply don't look right. This person should focus on specific types of invoices and purchase agreements looking for cost-saving opportunities. Here are eight potential actions for you to consider:

1. **Review invoices from your freight and shipping companies carefully, watching for inadvertent mistakes.** Most shippers are certainly honest and highly efficient, but when you ship millions of packages around the world daily, the odds are that at least some mistakes will be made. For instance, if a company has a customer who is located on Elm Drive and the shipper inadvertently enters the address as Elm Road, they might charge an additional fee of $5 for every package sent to this address. If an error has been made in entering a shipping address, the only way to ascertain this fact is to review the bill itself.

2. **Review lease agreements and lease bills.** If you lease any type of equipment, recognize that these lease agreements contain fine print that can cost you money. For instance, we paid a lease on a floor scrubber for a year and a half after the lease period had ended. What had happened was that during our lease period, the lease had been sold to another company, which had fine print in the contract stipulating that if we didn't inform them that we no longer wanted the floor scrubber, we would continue to be billed for it—which we were. As a result, we had the most expensive floor scrubber on the planet. Read your lease agreements and bills carefully and add notes to the file and to your calendar identifying exactly when leases are set to end. At that point, you can decide if you want to extend the lease or if you want to notify the leasing company that you're finished leasing the equipment.

3. **Make sure you are taking advantage of tax-exempt status.** Supplies for operating your business should be exempt from state sales tax. Some suppliers may not realize that your purchase is being used in your production and, consequently, may add sales tax to the invoice. This added charge can be

as much as 6.5 to 7 percent, so watch carefully to ensure that your company pays only as much tax as necessary.

4. **Read the fine print for all product and service purchases before making the purchases.** This is a tedious chore, so if you don't want to do it yourself, have a detail-oriented employee in your company take care of it. Most small business owners have a horror story about failing to read an agreement carefully and then in hindsight—and after a financial loss—wishing they had been more diligent. We negotiated a deal to reduce the monthly cost on a maintenance contract for a piece of equipment, and a year passed before someone brought it to my attention that we were still being billed at the old, higher rate. When we complained to our sales rep, he pointed out a clause in the agreement stating that disputes over billing had to be dealt with immediately. In other words, when we received a monthly bill with the higher rate, we should have contacted him right then, and we would have received a lower rate. Because we waited a year, we were out of luck.

5. **Make sure the numbers add up.** In other words, make sure you're getting the right quantity for what you're paying. Whenever you're dealing with a quantity purchase—1,001 push pins, 548 tie rods, 25,000 brochures—the possibility of error exists, so don't take the numbers for granted. At the very least, do a rough estimate to determine whether you're being overcharged. For instance, an invoice we received from a bottled gas supplier listed 52 gas bottles for which we were being charged a monthly rental fee. That number didn't seem right, and when we did a count, we realized we had only 41 bottles. This was another instance in which the supplier would go back only three months to give us credit for the wrong billing. Again, the fine print on the invoice said that the charges were valid unless they were disputed within a certain period of time. Over the course of a year,

this oversight cost us about $300. These types of mistakes happen all the time, and they aren't malicious but are simply the result of carelessness or misunderstandings.

6. **Scan your phone bills for money-saving tips.** Your telephone invoices are more valuable than you might think. From them, you can determine

- whether your employees are spending an excessive amount of time on the phone;
- whether your 800 number is being used—or abused;
- who is making the most expensive calls monthly;
- whether your employees are still using old long-distance calling cards, which can be very expensive; and
- whether the phone company has included erroneous charges.

If you can't determine the answers to these questions by reviewing your phone bill, then you need to request a more detailed invoice. If you're using a broker for local and long distance service, then you probably receive a highly detailed bill. If you have difficulty understanding your invoice, have a representative from your phone company stop in and explain the statement to you. It's likely that you have at least one employee who is racking up significant charges by making personal calls. It's also likely that another employee is unknowingly costing the company more than necessary on business calls—perhaps by using a long-distance calling card that costs 43 cents per minute, instead of a disposable calling card that costs only 4 cents per minute. Sometimes, employees simply need to be informed about how much their phone time is costing the company for them to modify their behaviors and save the company money.

Our long-distance invoices are sorted by the time of day the call was made, the length of each call, the number that was called or that a call came from, the top ten numbers called and received, and the ten most expensive calls by phone number. If you want to know if your employees are wasting valuable time on the phone or you want your broker to find a new phone service that better meets your needs, this invoice is your ticket for doing so.

7. **Check your health insurance invoices for currency and accuracy.** When reviewing a recent invoice from our provider, we discovered that we were still paying a significant amount for insurance coverage for a few employees who had quit months ago. Even though we had informed the insurance provider that they had quit, it had neglected to remove them from coverage. Many health insurance companies are bureaucratic and may be slow to update their records, so go over their invoices with a special degree of care.

8. **Appeal your legal bills when appropriate.** Law firms tend to be much better than some other service providers when it comes to accurate billing, but if a law firm makes a mistake, it can be an expensive one. Most small business owners use law firms for one purpose or another, and almost all of them have found and successfully appealed errors on their bills. Sometimes the error is an excessive amount of time billed for a relatively simple or minor matter. Sometimes it's a more blatant mistake—you're charged for a service that wasn't performed at all. Most firms are willing to listen and negotiate these mistakes. While they're not going to bend if they spent 100 hours defending you in a major environmental lawsuit, they may be willing to accept that charging you $500 for a copy of a transcript is excessive and reduce their fee.

PAPER MONEY: SAVING TIME, CLERICAL COSTS, AND THE ENVIRONMENT

The paperless office remains an ideal rather than a reality, especially for small companies that have not made a concerted effort to switch many of their functions from manual to electronic. If you're the owner of a small business or a top executive, however, you may not be aware of how much paper every transaction produces, as well as how much of your employees' time this paperwork consumes.

I discovered these costly facts of life when we changed our business operating system. We learned that we were generating an average of 15 pieces of paper daily to complete a transaction: the production order, invoices, shipping documents, order confirmations, and purchase requisitions. We worked hard at reducing this number to nine, taking steps such as faxing confirmations from our computers and reducing the standard three to four copies for invoicing to one. By taking these and other actions, we ended up saving $6,000 annually in both paper costs and reductions in time-intensive copying and filing. This took place eight years ago, so a few simple changes have saved the company at least $48,000 to date.

Most small businesses can save a similar amount of money by making a concerted effort to reduce their paper-per-transaction figures. You may find it helpful to put young, open-minded, computer-savvy people in charge of this task. Veteran employees tend to have a more-copies-the-better attitude. They have spent years operating under the assumption that paperwork is vital, that it provides legal protection, and that it is essential for the company to operate efficiently. Expect a certain amount of resistance from at least some of these individuals when you attempt to reduce your paper requirements. What I've found, however, is that once the new system is up and running and the paperwork load is reduced, people quickly become accustomed to the new system and recognize that the world won't end if you don't have copies in triplicate.

Perhaps your biggest obstacle to overcome is moving from mailed paper invoices to faxed or e-mailed ones. Psychologically, people resist making this transition; they may feel as if an invoice isn't official unless it's printed on paper and arrives by mail. To help you overcome this type of resistance, let me suggest three compelling reasons to switch to electronic invoicing:

1. You don't have to waste time addressing and stuffing envelopes.
2. You can save thousands of dollars on postage. Let's say you send 400 invoices monthly. That's 4,800 invoices annually, and at 39 cents per envelope, that comes out to over $1,850.
3. You can improve your cash flow. It takes at least a few days for mailed invoices to reach customers. If your receivables average $900,000 and 48 days at any given time and you reduce this by 3 days, you can improve your cash flow by more than $50,000.

If you're still worried that your customers won't take electronic invoices seriously, make it excessively clear that you have replaced your paper invoicing system entirely. In big, bold letters at the top of the electronic invoice, write:

"THIS IS INVOICE #XXXXX. THIS IS THE ONLY NOTIFICATION YOU WILL BE RECEIVING FOR THIS BILL. PLEASE REMIT IN 30 DAYS."

GIVE CREDIT, TAKE CREDIT

You may be among the many small companies that refuse to accept credit card payments because you don't want to pay a bank fee, pay the credit card company fee, or extend the wait to receive your money from a customer. This refusal, however, probably ends up costing you more money in the long run than you lose in the short run because of lost orders.

Consider that credit cards can be a safeguard against bad checks. The vast majority of your customers won't send you a bad check, but over a year or two, you're likely to receive at least one bad one. Credit cards are also a good alternative method if a customer's credit is shaky and you suspect that they may not be able to pay. Rather than suggesting a COD arrangement, offer to let them pay their bills by credit card.

To compensate your company for the time and money lost by accepting credit card payments, charge your customers an additional 3 percent for the privilege. Many small business owners may be reluctant to include this surcharge, fearing that customers will react badly. I'm sure they won't jump for joy when you inform them of this 3 percent additional charge, but most of them will accept it.

A few years ago, we were having some friends over to the house to watch a football game, and I realized we had very little in the house for our guests to eat or drink. I drove over to a small convenience store down the road right before the game to get what we needed. I gathered everything we would need, placed it on the counter, and realized I didn't have enough cash to pay for everything. When I took out my credit card, the cashier told me that the store levied an additional 3 percent charge for credit card purchases. I was more than a little surprised by this, and I suppose I was initially resentful. But I quickly decided that this was a convenient purchase, and for this convenience, I was willing to pay the relatively small additional amount to pay by credit card.

TWO PAYROLL OPTIONS THAT PAY OFF

Payroll systems tend to be difficult to change. You may have done your payroll one way for so long that it seems impossible to adjust even the smallest detail. Outsourcing this function, therefore, may seem out of the question. Many small business owners insisted that initially, they couldn't conceive of outsourcing this task. They worried about taking major responsibilities away from human resource or financial staff; they also worried about the fees charged by outside payroll companies. A significant percentage of them, though, overcame this reluctance to outsource when they realized that they could not only save money but that their key financial employees could add more value by devoting their talents to more important tasks. However, many business owners considering this switch don't know where to start. Here are a few first steps:

1. **Determine whether your payroll employees are making the best use of their time.** Do you have an accounting staff dedicated to and skilled at payroll tasks? Many small companies don't. As a result, your controller or other financial staff members are spending a great deal of time generating payroll checks. Are there other tasks that they're neglecting? In many small companies, the controller and finance staff are also in charge of the HR functions of the business. If you outsource payroll, it allows these people more time to devote to the HR functions of the business, which are often neglected.

2. **Ask your controller to contact at least three outside firms and secure quotes from each.** Remember, firm fees and services vary considerably. Make sure you're comparing apples to apples.

3. **Create a list of outsourcing pros and cons based on this information.** Assess what advantages besides the obvious labor savings will result. Will the firm provide timelier, easier to read reports? Will they minimize errors? Will they provide direct deposit and other options for employees?

4. **Make a decision based on current information.** The industry has changed considerably in the last four years. Costs have come down, and newer, computerized systems are

much more efficient. If you performed an analysis even two or three years ago, you're operating on outdated information.

The second payroll tactic involves switching to less frequent payroll runs for hourly employees—every other week rather than weekly. When we made this switch, we immediately reduced our annual payroll costs by $3,500. Recognize, however, that if you're contemplating a similar move, you might meet with some resistance. If you have employees who are accustomed to receiving their paycheck weekly, and especially if they've been receiving it that frequently from your company for many years, you need to facilitate this transition.

You can do so by talking to your employees about how this action will save the company money and will benefit them in the long run, but this argument may fall on deaf ears. A better facilitation strategy involves offering them something tangible in return for going along with this change. When we made this transition, we offered our people a short-term loan of up to $400. Though only two of our employees took us up on this offer, the gesture was appreciated by most of our staff and helped them better accept the change.

WORKING OUT WORKERS' COMPENSATION ISSUES

Obviously, there's only so much you can do to keep a lid on these costs. Even if you do everything possible to make sure your workplace is safe, people still can get injured on the job and your rates can skyrocket. Still, many small businesses are reactionary rather than proactive when it comes to workers' compensation, adopting a fatalistic or cynical attitude. As a result, they end up taking actions—or not taking actions—that cost them a lot of money. To be proactive and save some money in this area, here are some suggestions:

- **Settle all claims as quickly as possible.** The faster you remove a claim from your incident history, the better chance you have of keeping your rates down. In fact, in certain situations, you should seriously consider paying someone a bit more than you think they deserve to settle quickly. Of course, you should always consult a knowledgeable professional before making this type of decision, but from a purely cost-conscious perspective, settling is usually better than fighting.

- **Be aware of the variety of potential sources of professional advice.** Many excellent workers' compensation lawyers are available to offer advice on these cases. In certain situations, however, you should consider less expensive alternatives. You may have questions about specific incidents or policies that don't require a $300-per-hour attorney. We've found that as a member of the local Employee Resource Association, we've received excellent advice. You may have access to similar resources through membership in local or national professional associations.

- **Set up an information-gathering process to be implemented when accidents occur.** Information is money: establish a process that launches whenever an accident occurs, even if it doesn't seem particularly serious. Make sure employees who were around the area where the accident took place are interviewed. Take pictures of the accident area and date them. In addition, anyone involved in an accident should be tested for alcohol and drugs; this should be incorporated into your company policies.

- **Shop for a better workers' compensation policy every two or three years.** The easiest way to do this is to talk to other small businesses in your area and ask what they pay for workers' comp. Rates do change, and it's very easy to miss reductions if you're not proactive. There are also special programs that you can enroll in and qualify for reductions.

In Ohio, the Bureau of Workers' Compensation offers a random drug testing program, and companies who implement this program receive rate reductions. You should check your state workers' compensation agency to see if it offers a similar program.

13

INDIRECT STRATEGIES TO GENERATE SAVINGS

A great small business savings plan is holistic: it allows the savvy CEO to consider the full range of possibilities when it comes to running a company cost-consciously. Rather than focusing just on direct savings tactics such as shopping around and negotiating, small business owners need to think in broader terms, considering indirect methods to save money.

In this chapter, I want to present some of the best indirect methods that small business owners can implement to save money. As you'll see, some of them are relatively simple, quick actions, while others are a bit more complicated and longer term; some require adopting a new way of thinking about some aspect of the business, while others suggest you practice business methods that you've never practiced before.

These approaches can be challenging, at least in the sense that they require a certain amount of faith and patience. One of the suggestions, for instance, involves implementing performance reviews for hourly employees. This may seem like a huge administrative hassle with an uncertain reward. However, once the review system is in place, the administrative hassle will seem minor, and you'll be rewarded with superior performance from people who traditionally underperform. It's just that you don't see this reward surface immediately, nor can you measure it the way you can your monthly electric bill savings by turning out unnecessary lights. In many ways, though, these uncertain rewards can be larger and have a greater impact on your business' profitability than some shorter-term, direct-saving tactics.

PLAN TO SAVE MONEY

Years ago, my wife suggested that I attend a class that taught planning skills so that I could become better organized. She knew that I wrote to-do lists on pads of paper and then rewrote them each day, carrying over the tasks that didn't get done from one list to the next. This crude system was better than no system at all, but it wasn't particularly efficient and didn't offer the degree of sophistication necessary to run a small business in an optimum manner.

Still, I resisted taking this class and continued to rely on my extremely low-tech approach until my production manager bought and began using a day planner. As you may know, production managers often have trouble staying focused and organized because of the many demands on their time and the curves thrown at them. In the production manager's performance reviews, I had mentioned that he should attempt to become better organized and use his time more effectively.

When the production manager bought his planner, we paid for him to take classes in how to use it. It turned out to be one of the best investments we ever made in improving an employee's performance. While he was a good performer before he began to use the planner, he became a superior performer afterward. Tasks that might have slipped between the cracks before were now caught. He maximized just about every minute of his time and made sure the entire production department ran smoothly and met all its deadlines.

The improvement in his performance convinced me to purchase a day planner and invest the time to learn to use it efficiently, and the only thing I regret is that I didn't buy one 15 years earlier.

Today, 16 of our managerial employees use these planners, and the company pays for classes in how best to utilize a day planner; we also pay for refill pages for the planners. These costs are nothing compared to the benefits, which include:

- **Reducing wasted time.** I don't know how to calculate what wasted employee time means in dollars, but it is a huge loss. Most employees don't waste time because they're lazy, uncaring, or pursuing their own personal agendas. They waste time because they're disorganized and don't maximize their efficiency. No one has ever taught them how to organize their time, and this is exactly what a day planner does.

- **Meeting tough deadlines.** How many times in the last year has one of your employees expressed concern over meeting a deadline? How many times has an individual or team disappointed you by failing to meet a key one? "Too often" is the common answer. The key to meeting a tight deadline is usually nothing more than creating a plan as soon as you receive the assignment. Many times, people procrastinate, don't plan at all, and realize too late that they haven't spent enough hours or brought in enough resources to meet a deadline. When deadlines are approached in a systematic way right from the beginning, the odds are that they will be met.

- **Sealing the cracks that things fall into.** Even in the smallest of businesses, certain responsibilities fall through the cracks. This is because people are overwhelmed with key tasks and are under pressure to accomplish these tasks. Most of the time, this neglect isn't willful or malicious. It's just that there are only so many things people can keep track of in their heads. With a day planner to assist them, however, these secondary but important tasks remain visible. They may be placed on the back burner temporarily, but they don't get lost in the jumble of other activities, and it's more likely that they will be attended to.

OFFER SPENDING FREEDOM

The financial empowerment of key employees can save your company money. This statement may seem counterintuitive, but many small businesses suffer from micromanaging CEOs who make their employees fearful about spending anything at all on their own. When employees feel disempowered in this way, they rarely make astute decisions involving purchases. They don't take advantage of a deal as soon as it surfaces, feeling that they must get permission or go through a certain procedure before taking action. As a result, they often miss out on the deal. Similarly, many small business managers believe that trying to save the company money isn't their responsibility; they see financial issues as outside of their authority.

You should attempt to change this attitude. Almost uniformly, the small business owners who said that their top employees were highly cost-conscious and financially astute gave these people at least some spending discretion. These executives didn't have to check with the boss before making buying or other financial decisions. This doesn't mean they were given carte blanche to spend whatever they wanted whenever they wanted. However, giving your staff the freedom to make financial decisions and purchases valued at less than $1,000 without your approval demonstrates a certain amount of trust and encourages responsible spending. As a result, they will not only save you some money but some time—you have, in effect, transferred lower-level but time-consuming financial decision making to your key employees.

If you're uncomfortable giving this amount of financial freedom to your staff, recognize that you have a built-in safeguard to avoid poor financial decision making. Your employees should know that you're going to review the account payable statements carefully, and the last thing they want is to have an ill-advised purchase called to their attention.

POST COLORFUL NOTES

I've discussed the importance of encouraging people to save money and suggested specific incentives you might use in this regard. These incentives, however, don't always need to be formal rewards. Over the years, I've used different colors of sticky notes (I currently favor lime-green) to compliment employees who initiate a particularly inventive or valuable cost-saving action. I stick the notes in their work areas so that they are impossible to miss. I suppose it's the equivalent of a grade school teacher who gives a student a gold star for doing well on a project, but people seem to appreciate these small accolades. I try to write a personal message of appreciation on the notes to convey why I found the employee's contribution so valuable.

If you are skeptical about how your employees might respond to these notes, let me share the story of a controller who worked for me for a number of years. He was very bright and had helped the company save money in many different ways, and I was fond of leaving sticky notes on his computer terminal. When he received an offer he couldn't refuse from another company, he came to my office for the exit interview, and in his hand was every note I had ever given him. He told me how much those notes meant to him, and over the years, other employees have told me the same thing.

Taking the time to write out a note may be one of the smallest investments you can make, and it can yield a huge return in terms of boosting morale and facilitating communication with your employees.

DO HOURLY EMPLOYEE REVIEWS

Conducting reviews is a time-consuming process; it also opens the doors to complaints and requests for raises. You may believe that it's difficult enough to do reviews for your professional staff, and the last thing you want is to conduct reviews for all your employees.

While I understand this reaction, my personal experience has been that the positives far outweigh the negatives. We've been doing reviews for hourly employees for nine years, and it has worked out to the benefit of both management and these hourly employees. If you set up the review system so that you limit the time required, you will probably find that the system will create much more productive hourly employees.

- **Create and distribute review sheets for employees to complete before their review.** These review sheets should be simple and easy to complete. They should basically ask your employees to tell you what they believe their major contributions and strengths were during the past year, as well as their weaknesses and failures. Based on this review, you simply need to assess what they've written and determine whether you agree.
- **Limit the actual reviews to 15 minutes.** Make sure your employees know that this is the maximum time they'll receive. This knowledge encourages them to use the time well and focus on the most important challenges or achievements they've dealt with in the previous year.

- **Make sure you or another top executive are present.** This isn't a task you should routinely hand off. Of course, there are times when the owner will be unable to attend these reviews because of more pressing matters, but a top executive should be present at every review. This ensures that the review will be taken seriously.
- **Take action based on the outcome of the review.** This doesn't just mean giving people a raise or praise if they have a positive review (though this is certainly appropriate). Taking action also means responding to what you learn from the review sheet and the 15-minute session. For example, during one review, we discovered that one of our clerical employees had prior AutoCAD programming experience and was interested in developing his knowledge in this area and backing up our programmer. We paid for this employee to take an additional course in AutoCAD, and we now have the security of knowing that he can provide a great backup for our programmer if necessary.

These reviews are not designed to reward or punish people but to foster a sense of inclusiveness. Employees who feel that you're paying attention to them are much more likely to pay attention to their work. They will make fewer mistakes and contribute more ideas that are good. A simple, easy-to-use review process can result in this outcome. If it does, you'll find that the time and effort invested are more than worth it.

HIRE LOCAL STUDENTS

Hiring local high school and college students can not only provide you with an inexpensive source of part-time labor, but it can also supply the company with value-adding skills that it might not otherwise possess. Most obviously, younger people often have computer skills that other employees might lack. They may be computer science majors or simply be avidly pursuing it as a hobby, but they often are aware of new, breakthrough products and how to employ software to produce the best possible results. Of course, students aren't at the level of a good MIS or other technical person, but they are often quite adept at Internet research or overcoming e-commerce obstacles. Take advantage of their high-tech skills. They may save you the cost of a professional consultant or provide you with a fix that your own employees haven't thought of.

A student worker might also possess artistic skills that you can capitalize on. Perhaps you need a new logo or help with a Web site design. Professional artists are often quite expensive, and students may have sufficient artistic talent for your purposes at a much lower price tag.

Perhaps the best reason to hire local students, however, is that they help you establish a good relationship with your community. Some of these students are sons and daughter of prominent people in town, and by hiring them for summer jobs or part-time positions during the school year, you forge a link with a community member who may be able to assist you in some way. One student's parent may be on the town's zoning board and help you clear some obstacles when you need a zoning variance to construct a new factory. Another student may have a parent who is a prospective customer. A "hire local" policy also marks you as a good neighbor in the eyes of the community. It means that your neighbors may be more willing to do what they can to keep you happy.

Finally, most small business owners who have set up internship programs for college students interested in some aspect of business have been extremely pleased with the results, noting that not only did they have the services of a smart, energetic future MBA for a summer, but that at least some of these interns applied for jobs and were hired when they graduated. The internships really served as apprenticeships and were a cost-effective recruiting tool for their business.

NETWORK WITH OTHER BUSINESS OWNERS

This seems like an obvious piece of advice, but many CEOs of small companies rarely, if ever, interact with other business owners. While they attend trade shows for their industries and have plenty of chances to talk to other owners on the trade-show floor or in seminars and workshops, they don't take advantage of these opportunities. Perhaps they neglect to do so because they feel that outsiders don't know their business. Perhaps they are afraid of giving away competitive information. Whatever the reason, they are missing out on a chance to acquire knowledge that translates into both profits and dollars saved.

Other business owners face very similar issues in terms of employee morale, hiring, recruiting, budgeting, and other concerns. Even if they're in a completely different industry, they will probably be able to offer you advice on at least some topics that are relevant to your particular situation. Just as importantly, other small business owners can refer you to prospective customers, tell you about prospective hires, and educate you about both good and bad suppliers. They also provide you with someone to talk to who is in your position. Many small business owners complain that no one understands their problems, that their employees and outside advisors don't really get the issues they're grappling with. By networking with other small business owners, you have a chance to engage in conversations with your peers. Even if it doesn't lead to solutions, it will help reduce your stress level and make it just a bit easier for you to function effectively.

In your area, you probably have at least a few organizations that give you access to other small business owners. Here are a few of these groups:

- **Employer Association Group** (EAG; *www.eagnet.nam.org*). I'm a member of this manufacturers' group, and they've saved me a lot of money over the years, as I've mentioned in previous chapters. They specialize in human resources-related issues (hiring, firing, supervisor training, benefits, discipline) and offer forums for owner-to-owner interactions. For instance, they hold a CEO roundtable meeting every other month. In our group, 12 people assemble for a two-hour breakfast meeting and discuss current issues related to operating our businesses. I always come away from these meetings with at least one good idea that I want to implement.

- **Chief Executive Boards International** (CEBI; *www.chiefex ecutiveboards.com*). This is another group of which I have been a member for nearly ten years; it has helped me a great deal. Local boards of approximately 12 members meet quarterly for an entire day. We share our problems in the hope that other members have experienced similar problems and can offer potential solutions. Members also share their successes at each meeting, providing fresh ideas and tools. CEBI essentially functions as your own informal board of directors. In addition, CEBI facilitates a summit conference where members from around the country gather for a two-day meeting. In these national board meetings, members again share their positive and negative experiences.
- **Young Presidents' Organization** (YPO; *www.ypo.org*). This group is for business owners younger than 45. It is a very well-run organization with many supportive forums. They also bring in speakers to address specific issues during conferences and meetings. Most major cities have a YPO chapter.
- **Vistage** (formerly TEC International; *www.vistage.com*) is another organization that offers networking opportunities for business owners. Its programs incorporate regular meetings with peers, executive coaching resources, speakers and workshops, and an online resource library for members.

Other possibilities include Rotary Clubs or chambers of commerce. Both organizations provide you with the chance to network with other business owners and potentially learn from their mistakes rather than your own, and as you know, your mistakes can cost the company a considerable amount of money.

FIND THINGS TO DO OUTSIDE OF YOUR BUSINESS

This money-saving suggestion requires a leap of faith, but I think you'll find it has merit. Over the years, you've probably known at least one person who owned a small business and was a workaholic. This person may have worked extremely hard and been a very good executive, but the odds are, the workaholic's myopia hurt the business. This owner may have been obsessed with work to the point of micromanaging everyone and everything. It is very easy for this person to think that a workaholic approach profits the company. In reality, it creates losses. Workaholic business owners often are cheap without being intelligently frugal; they resent every penny they have to pay to others and fail to invest in good people and equipment. They are so focused on the little details that they never focus on future goals—especially ways to save money in the long term rather than the short term.

If you are this person, I would urge you to establish a life outside of the business. Whether that means spending more time with your family, taking up golf, enrolling in a class, or going hiking, the key is to spend quality time outside of the office. As much as my partner and I love our business, we make it a point to take at least four weeks of vacation annually. We have family, friends, and interests that provide a balance between our personal and professional lives.

How does this help your business save money? Here are two ways:

1. **It allows you to analyze expenses objectively.** If you're at work all the time (not just physically, but mentally), then it's difficult to see an expense as anything but a drain on the business. You may end up cutting all spending to the bare minimum, which is like cutting off your nose to spite your face. As you know, a successful small business owner cuts costs not with an axe but with intelligence and discretion. The old adage is true: sometimes you have to spend money to make money. When you're too close to the business, you can't tell what is a good expense and what is a bad one.

2. **It allows you to look at profit and loss with a clear, calm mind.** If the business is everything to you, you measure your worth based on profit and loss. This means that you have no tolerance for temporary financial setbacks, and you panic when you lose a customer or have to replace an expensive machine part. This panic reaction may cause you to downsize unnecessarily to reduce costs, in the process losing key employees, which will hurt your business in the long run. A balanced life, therefore, gives you the ability to think in both the short term and the long term and to weigh risk against reward. Ultimately, this results in better leadership and management and helps you to avoid costly mistakes.

SO MUCH TO SAVE, SO LITTLE TIME TO SAVE IT

As you think about the wide range of suggestions offered throughout this book, you may feel overwhelmed. Given all of your responsibilities, how will you find the hours in the day to do hourly employee reviews, catch mistakes in invoices, or even create colorful notes for individual employees? Perhaps an even greater obstacle to implementing the suggestions found in these pages is inertia. The thought of revamping the way you reward salespeople or creating a new policy for credit card usage may weary you; you anticipate the objections, the need for all sorts of paperwork and research, and you wonder if it's really worth it.

It is.

Still, I recognize the realities of running a small business and know that when a key employee quits or a piece of machinery breaks, everything beyond fixing the problem gets put on the back burner. When the crisis passes, so too does your resolve to save money in new and different ways. You're so exhausted from dealing with the emergency that you don't want to place a big new responsibility on your plate.

There are ways for you to make this whole process a bit easier to implement and manage, keeping you motivated even as you maintain your day-to-day job responsibilities. To that end, here are some recommendations.

Create a written savings plan. Formalizing a plan increases the odds of its being implemented. Go through this book and jot down the ideas that most appeal to you. After each idea, write an action step. Don't list a general action, such as "Consider changing purchasing protocols so that we shop around among suppliers." Instead, write, "Talk to Joe, head of purchasing, and ask him to create a new shop-around protocol for dealing with suppliers."

Limit the plan to five key ideas that you think will help your company the most. Then prioritize acting on these ideas and follow that order in implementing them.

Once you've successfully implemented your top five ideas, create a new plan with five more new ideas.

Go on to the next savings approach when the current one isn't working. Don't become stuck or frustrated. You may discover that no matter what you do, you are unable to cut significant dollars from your equipment purchases—that your employees are already doing the best possible job in keeping these costs low. Instead of spending time and energy in an area where further savings simply may not be possible, go on to the next tactic—I've listed many for you to choose from. In this way, you won't try one thing, decide it doesn't work, and go back to your wasteful ways.

Keep a running tab of money saved. This measurement is crucial. It will provide you with the motivation to invest the time and energy to save money. Once you know that all your effort is saving you $2,000 monthly, you'll overcome the inertia discussed earlier. Although some of the recommendations in this book result in savings that are hard to quantify, do try to estimate the money you've saved. Have one column for tangible dollars saved and another column for estimated savings. If you find it difficult to assign a number to a specific benefit—such as what you gain when distributing colorful notes to employees—write an intangible benefit ("Elise seems much more enthusiastic about her job since I started putting notes on her computer").

Share these ideas with your management team. There is no way you can implement all these suggestions on your own. Other people in your organization are in better positions to implement certain tactics than you are. Encourage them to test some of the suggestions here. Ask them to come up with their own money-saving concepts based on their knowledge of a certain area. The ideas in these pages can inspire them to come up with better, more germane plans; they don't have to follow them to the letter.

Create a long-term plan after you've accomplished a few short-term ones. Once you get the hang of saving money—and once you see the benefits—you'll find it easier to be more ambitious in your planning. Ideally, you'll build up to 50 or more money-saving tactics—you'll be taking action to save money in purchasing, in employee benefits, in credit card usage, in sales, and in other areas. This is when the savings really add up. When you're saving $2,000 here and $5,000 there, the total dollar amount becomes staggering. This isn't going to happen overnight, so there's no need to create this long-term plan right at the start. When you have some successful short-term plans under your belt, though, you're probably ready to create a more ambitious savings plan.

How much can a small company save? I suppose that depends on how much waste a company is guilty of. No doubt, some small companies spend money as if they'll never run out. Perhaps they experienced skyrocketing success at first, and it seemed as if they could spend freely without ever experiencing problems. Then the downturn hit. For a company like this, huge opportunities exist to save hundreds of thousands of dollars.

At the same time, I believe even the typical cost-conscious small company has significant opportunities to save. When you start asking yourself the tough questions this book poses and look at saving in a holistic sense, you'll realize that even if you're frugal in some areas, you aren't as diligent about keeping costs down in other areas.

My goal in writing this book was to share the tools and techniques that other small business owners and I have found to be useful in spending and saving wisely. I fully believe that this advice, combined with your determination to put it into practice, will help you reach whatever financial goals you set for yourself and for your company.

For more cost-saving ideas, straight from readers like you, check out *www.thesmallbusinesssavingsplan.com*.

Tim Gase has spent the past ten years working for Peerless Saw Company, a small manufacturing business, in Groveport, Ohio, the last seven years as co-owner. During that time, he helped grow the business from a $6.8 million company to one worth more than $10 million, dramatically improving the company's bottom line and net profit.

Prior to joining Peerless, Gase worked for Apex, a division of Cooper Industries, a $4 billion company, where he held eight positions over a 12-year period, including business manager for three product lines with P&L responsibility for about $7 million in sales. He has an MBA from Ohio University.

With products serving children, adults, schools and businesses, Kaplan has an educational solution for every phase of learning.

KIDS AND SCHOOLS

SCORE! Educational Centers offer individualized tutoring programs in reading, math, writing and other subjects for students ages 4-14 at more than 160 locations across the country. We help students achieve their academic potential while developing self-confidence and a love of learning. *www.escore.com*

We also partner with schools and school districts through Kaplan K12 Learning Services to provide instructional programs that improve results and help all students achieve. We support educators with professional development, innovative technologies, and core and supplemental curriculum to meet state standards. *www.kaplank12.com*

TEST PREP AND ADMISSIONS

Kaplan Test Prep and Admissions prepares students for more than 80 standardized tests, including entrance exams for secondary school, college and graduate school, as well as English language and professional licensing exams. We also offer private tutoring and one-on-one admissions guidance. *www.kaptest.com*

HIGHER EDUCATION

Kaplan Higher Education offers postsecondary programs in fields such as business, criminal justice, health care, education, and information technology through more than 70 campuses in the U.S. and abroad, as well as online programs through Kaplan University and Concord Law School. *www.khec.com • www.kaplan.edu • www.concordlawschool.edu*

PROFESSIONAL

If you are looking to start a new career or advance in your field, Kaplan Professional offers training to obtain and maintain professional licenses and designations in the accounting, financial services, real estate and technology industries. We also work with businesses to develop solutions to satisfy regulatory mandates for tracking and compliance. *www.kaplanprofessional.com*

Kaplan helps individuals achieve their educational and career goals. We build futures one success story at a time.